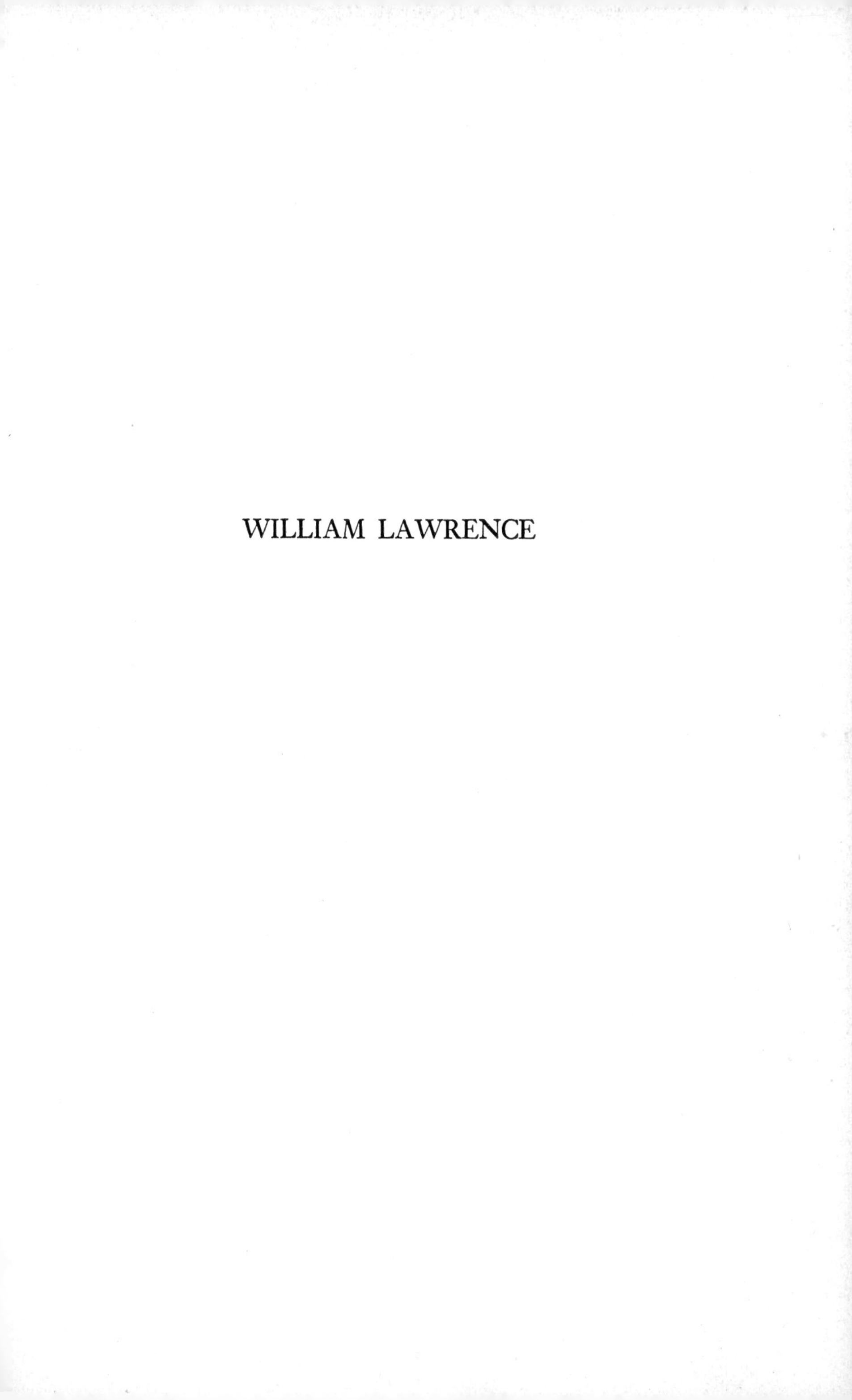

WILLIAM LAWRENCE

LONDON : HUMPHREY MILFORD
OXFORD UNIVERSITY PRESS

THE RIGHT REVEREND WILLIAM LAWRENCE, D.D., LL.D.
On His Eightieth Birthday, May 30, 1930

WILLIAM LAWRENCE

Later Years of a Happy Life

BY

HENRY KNOX SHERRILL

CAMBRIDGE : MASSACHUSETTS
HARVARD UNIVERSITY PRESS
1943

PRINTED AT THE HARVARD UNIVERSITY PRINTING OFFICE
CAMBRIDGE, MASSACHUSETTS, U.S.A.

Preface

IN 1926, Bishop Lawrence's autobiography, "*Memories of a Happy Life*," was published, and received an enthusiastic welcome. No doubt at the time he felt that the task had been completed, but he lived on for almost fifteen years of varied and happy experience.

The purpose of this book is to finish the story. The Bishop's friends may welcome an additional reminder of a greatly loved and admired associate. Those who did not know him personally, but enjoyed his autobiography, may be interested to follow him on the last lap of the journey of life. His words were wise, based on a rare combination of high idealism and practical common sense. His addresses in these later years stand on their own feet, and are pertinent to our times. We can well heed his advice touching many fields of activity, from current trends in Church and State to the use of the voice, in two short articles every speaker would do well to read. In many other ways, his long experience of life will prove helpful. Then there is that group of people who must face retirement, and take their place, as they are apt to describe it, "on the shelf." Admitting, as Bishop Lawrence always did, that he possessed special advantages, nevertheless his years of useful and happy retirement can be a source of stimulation and of inspiration to those who have felt with dismay that their active and useful days had come to an end.

So far as has been possible, I have tried to have the Bishop tell the story in his own words. This preserves the continuity with his autobiography; and the Bishop wrote and spoke with a certain freshness and vitality which are lost in reproduction. While these years were active for one of his age, of course the great events of his life took place before his retirement. In this period, what he said is more important than what he did. Thus I make no apology for the great number of quotations from the Bishop's diary and from his addresses, for they present William Lawrence himself.

It must be admitted that these pages are written by a grateful and devoted friend. All my ministry, Bishop Lawrence has been a trusted guide, and no predecessor and successor could possibly have had happier relationships. But I do not think because this is true that I am a blind friend. With certain opinions of the Bishop I found difficulty: for example, I could never wholly understand his attitude toward the League of Nations; and, perhaps unfortunately, the Christian religion seems more complex to me than it did to him. Within my own limitations, in my opinion these pages present not a mere eulogy, but Bishop Lawrence as he was these later years. He was as clear as crystal. There were, so far as I have been able to discover, no hidden motives or obscure ambitions. Certainly there were no skeletons in the closet to be hidden from popular view.

I believe that even the most modern of so-called realistic biographers would find it difficult to make copy of the Bishop, for whether in public or in private, he was always the same, himself, a wise and experienced leader in Church and in State, yet withal a simple child of God and a devoted servant of his Master.

My thanks are due Dean Henry Bradford Washburn and Miss Marguerite Kimball for many valuable suggestions. Quotations from *Memories of a Happy Life* and *The New American* have been made by permission of Houghton Mifflin Company, the authorized publishers. The picture of Bishop Lawrence at the Harvard Tercentenary was generously made available by the Harvard Alumni Bulletin. I am indebted to various members of the Bishop's family for information, particularly in regard to the Bar Harbor scene. Especially I am grateful to my wife for constant helpfulness and encouragement.

HENRY KNOX SHERRILL

January 1, 1943

CONTENTS

ILLUSTRATIONS

WILLIAM LAWRENCE

I

The Retired Bishop

MAY 4, 1927 — 12. Convention at Ford Hall. I read my short address telling them of my resignation. Chas. replied with a few words. They all stood during our addresses. I gave blessing; then "O God our help" sung, and after shaking hands with Charles and Babcock, I slipped out. Very simple but very moving to us all. Stood at back of Hall and heard Freddie speak on student work; interesting that just after I made my farewell to the Convention he should be the first after me to speak. To Twentieth Century Club. Julia gave luncheon to one hundred and thirty wives of the clergy. I received with her and got them started. Home for nap: insane woman to see me: pretty tired, so went to see Cunningham,[1] who in his loneliness was cheerful. Came away feeling better. Evening: Copley Plaza. Dinner of Episcopalian Club, laymen and clergy: 550 at table. They gave me a great reception, long applause, and cheers both before and after I spoke. I spoke of gratitude as the great motive: of friendship and love, the pleasure in old age of being of help to individuals and of keeping in touch with the young. Washburn and one or two spoke, sad in fact that really the end of my work as Bishop of Massachusetts. A most happy day in the gratitude which the people seem to feel and their regret at my resignation. It is, I am sure, right and wise and I hope will set an example to other old Bishops to clear the way for younger men.

With this entry in his diary, Bishop Lawrence described the announcement of his resignation as Bishop, just thirty-

[1] An old retired clergyman, almost blind.

four years to the day from his election. In his address to the Convention [2] he stated, "I have always believed that a Body created to lead the people should be officered and administered by men in full vigor, and that old men should give way and resign office in order that young men should have full opportunity and authority; for without full authority, even though he may seldom use it, no man can really lead.

"The Churches in this country would in my judgment do more effective work and advance with stronger steps if this principle were observed. With this in mind I have presented for action by the House of Bishops the resignation of my jurisdiction and title as Bishop of Massachusetts by reason of age, although I am for my years in full vigor. . . .

"My term of office has been longer than that of any of my predecessors. During these thirty-four years, we, my dear Brethren of the Clergy and Laity, have worshipped and worked together in perfect harmony. There has not been a single note of discord; we have been and still are in the Unity of the Spirit and bond of peace.

"That this action is a hard one for me to take and is a real sacrifice I know that you will appreciate. That it is just, wise and right, I am sure you will agree. . . .

"May God's blessing rest upon you all."

As the Bishop walked out of Ford Hall that May morning he was deeply moved, as were the members of the Convention. For him, with the acceptance of his resignation within a few weeks by the House of Bishops, it marked the end of a responsibility and a routine which he had car-

[2] *The Church Militant*, May 1927.

ried for so long: for the members of the Convention it seemed to mean the close of an epoch. The Bishop had ordained many of them, and to all had been a counsellor and a guide.

Most people would have said that his active life had come to an end. Behind him were the many events described so vividly in his autobiography, *Memories of a Happy Life*:[3] the years of his ministry at Grace Church, Lawrence, when his experience of life widened and deepened as he came into close touch with people of every walk of life, his professorship and deanship in the Episcopal Theological School, with his intimate relationship to young men; and then the thirty-four years of his episcopate, with all the varied activities of Church and State at home and abroad. He was within a few weeks of his seventy-seventh birthday. Even though he had always been active, he had never been robust. At the time of his election as Bishop, he had hesitated to accept for this reason, and did so only after consultation with his family physician and a nerve specialist. Yet he was destined to live for almost fifteen years after his retirement, full of vitality and of interest in people and affairs. It might have been truly said of him, "Life begins at seventy-seven"; for at that age he began a new and significant phase of his long life of service. There are few men in any walk of life of whom this is true.

What were the assets he possessed in this new career of active retirement? Certainly they were great. He had the financial means to remove that usual burden upon old age, worry as to the ways and means of keeping the wolf from

[3] Houghton Mifflin Co., 1926.

the door. He was blessed with a large and happy family circle. He still retained his membership on the Harvard Corporation and the National Council of the Protestant Episcopal Church, his presidency of the Board of Trustees of St. Mark's and Groton schools, as well as the trusteeship of the family estate, and the presidency of the Church Pension Fund. He had many friends who turned to him constantly for advice, and there were innumerable charitable and civic organizations, not only in Boston but throughout the country, which came to him for counsel.

One of his greatest assets was that to the end he was spared the usual infirmities of old age. He had illnesses, many of them, including the whooping cough; he had recurrent difficulties with his heart; but his eyesight and hearing were apparently as good as ever. His voice, while not as strong, was clear, and could be depended upon for public addresses. His mind was as alert as that of a young man, with the added wisdom of almost four-score years of accumulated experience. Except for the tendency to indulge in reminiscence, which he did with great charm, he revealed none of the characteristics which are usually associated with old age.

This was true to a remarkable degree of his physical appearance. As he grew older, he seemed somewhat smaller, until he stepped forward to make an address at the Diocesan Convention or a Community Fund gathering. Then he would characteristically throw back his shoulders, and would seem as he did twenty years before. He had always been a handsome man, but as the years passed his face expressed to an increasing degree gentleness and serenity. On his birthday he wrote in his diary:

Seventy-seven years old, feel as I did at fifty or sixty, but not able to do as much at a stretch and of course do not run except short distances. Walk as fast as ever but not long at a stretch. Can work at desk and on chores morning, noon and night, but do not do it much. Three services a Sunday would probably use me up for the next day.

Certainly William Lawrence had much for which to be grateful, and he was always filled with gratitude. He ended his diaries each year almost without exception, with some such phrase as "More blessings have come to me through life than to anyone I know"; but many other men have had similar advantages and yet have found old age a burden. Outward circumstances, however favorable, cannot guarantee the inner resources of the spirit. Here was the Bishop's great achievement. He did more than endure old age: he made it a career of serene living and of happy service to others.

He possessed to a remarkable degree the spirit of youth. He wrote:

How old is Old Age? The Psalmist sets it at threescore years and ten. My experience is that some men are born old, they were never young, and while I have not consulted an expert on the subject, I am inclined to think there are some boys and girls, indeed some infants, who at birth lacked certain vitamins or powers or faculties, and have lacked them throughout, the possession of which really makes them normal and vigorous young men and women, and later old men and women. They have always been old. This vagueness as to the exact date of old age is emphasized also by the fact that as no two persons are just alike, no two old men have just the same kind of old age. A few years ago a friend of mine, some eighty years of age, sent me a copy of a little book on old age. I wrote thanking him, saying that I had read it carefully, and being about eighty myself, did not believe a word of it. His experience was not mine, his years evidently of labor and sorrow. Yet on the surface he was really a cheerful old man. Some old people think that they ought to feel old and a bit mournful. Again, my thoughtful friends urge, "But why not write your own experience of old age?" My answer is, "How do you know that I am old? The almanac and the certificate of birth may give a high figure, but I know old men and women who are a generation younger in years. When did my old age begin, if it has begun?" [4]

In one sense it never did begin. The Bishop found in general his contemporaries among those many years younger. He wrote in his diary:

> Lunch of Class of '71. I think ten were present — a mournful occasion. I think and wish they would give them up: however, I put all the pep into it that I could, talked probably more than half the time: half of them more or less deaf.

In an article which he prepared but never used, he wrote:

> Hence today while I do not make peremptory engagements, and never allow myself to be driven, I find that each day brings its interest, its varied companionship, its interesting problems of vocation and avocation. Meanwhile with an ever increasing family I am kept in touch with the younger people of all ages. Indeed I am startled to find that I have but two or three old friends living; scores have died, and two years ago I officially closed up the records of my Harvard Class of 1871 which graduated with one hundred and fifty men — at that time the largest in Harvard's history. "How depressing!" one says. Not a bit of it — it is all in the order of nature, and I have my part here still to play until God calls me.

He once referred to the point of view of a contemporary who had described the satisfactions of old age as being re-

[4] Many of the quotations on old age in this chapter are from a manuscript in the Bishop's hand found among his papers and marked "Worthless: never used."

moved from the heat and struggle of life, and of living with happy memories: "I never had one of those feelings any more than as if I were twenty-one years old."

The Bishop was cautious in his comments on the ways of the younger generation, lest, as he put it, he be dubbed a "cynical old man." The truth is, he loved youth because he was young in his own heart. He made a practice of inviting to dinner, from time to time, a group of seniors in the Episcopal Theological School. In this way he kept in touch with the younger clergy of the Church. He was delighted when young engaged couples came to see him, and especially pleased when he could write in his diary after the name of the bride-to-be, "attractive," as he frequently did. On many questions he was apparently more radical than younger men, not only because he was truly forward-looking, but because he could not bear to have anyone think he was conservative or cautious or conventional on account of being old in years. There was a freshness in his conversation as well as in his formal and informal addresses which was unique, and came from the freshness of youth within. He showed this spirit in his whole appearance. No one had greater natural dignity, but to the end there was a spring to his step and his entire bearing. He never walked like an old man. He disliked using the elevator which had been placed in 122 Commonwealth Avenue after his first heart attack, and insisted on walking up the steps whenever possible. His gray fedora hat, worn generally at somewhat of an angle, the gray suit, the turned-down collar and rather bright tie, the cane swinging in the air, the rather brisk pace — these were characteristic of the Bishop during his years of so-called retirement.

With the asset of youth, the Bishop had the faculty of happily putting off the old and on the new. "My conviction has always been," he said, "that when an executive officer has once resigned his office, he should thereafter take no part or even give the appearance of taking part in the administration of the office. I have seen parishes disrupted by the well-intentioned or unconscious interference of rectors who have resigned. My slogan has been, 'When I resign, I resign.'"

This principle the Bishop held to without any deviation, so far as administrative responsibility was concerned. He expressed it more informally in his speech at the luncheon following the consecration of Bishop Babcock's successor, Bishop Heron, when he turned to Bishop Babcock, for many years Suffragan Bishop, with the words, "Babcock, you and I are *out*." To a friend who came to ask his advice about resigning the treasurership of a college because of ill health, he said, "Yes, drop all responsibility immediately: assume that you are entering upon another phase of life and usefulness."

The secret was expressed in that note in the Bishop's diary on the day he told the Convention of his intention to resign: "I spoke of friendship and love, the pleasure in old age of being of help to individuals and of keeping in touch with the young." When William Lawrence was the active Bishop, he was pressed for time: he necessarily had to give judgments: he travelled constantly. He was sympathetic, of course, in emergencies, but he gave the impression of being the very efficient and somewhat reserved administrator of many affairs. He would not, with the exception of his old friend, Dr. Endicott Peabody, call any of the clergy of the Diocese by their first names. He was fearful of giving the impression of favoritism or of undue intimacy with the few, rather than the balanced relationship to the whole group. The moment he had resigned, all these imposed restrictions were off. He called his close friends of all ages by their first names at once. At the time of the acceptance of his resignation by the House of Bishops, he surprised a much younger friend and his wife by saying in high spirits, "No more 'Bishop,' – call me Bill." Needless to say, this was not done or meant to be done. The Bishop with all his informality and friendliness had a deep reserve of dignity. In Longwood, however, many of his contemporaries referred to him as "Willy Lawrence." Most of his family and a few friends called him "William." A letter from Judge Robert Grant, written shortly before the latter's death and kept in some papers of the Bishop's, began "Dear Bill."

With retirement, William Lawrence had time and strength for personal relationships with a large group of people. It was as if he had gone back to the old pastoral life of the Lawrence days. He called at hospitals and in homes whenever friends were ill, and brought his usual gift, a single rose; but more important, he came with understanding, sympathy and cheer. He wrote frequent notes in his own hand: "notes" is the proper word, as they were always short and to the point. The Bishop had a remarkable gift of conciseness. He could write a completely satisfying letter of thanks or of cheer on a calling card. Perhaps it was the fact of his reserve which, when broken, made the few words seem all the more. But it was true that to many people the words "Many thanks" or "Good address," signed by the initials "W. L.," meant more than pages written by someone else. These messages of encouragement and of friendship went out constantly to a wide circle of friends. When complimented on this facility of expression in compact form, he said, "Yes, but it took me seventy years to learn how."

After his resignation, the Bishop declined to meet with vestries of parishes, or with official representatives of diocesan organizations. When he was out, he was out. But his door was always open to friends desiring his advice. He would say, "Woke up in the morning, nothing on the calendar. By eleven o'clock the day is filled." He enjoyed this personal ministry. His interest was always in people and affairs rather than in books. At times the problems were difficult, and at the end of the day he would be tired, but on the whole they kept him going, on a new phase of life. He liked to feel that he was of use, and many times the very unexpectedness and informality of the call brought interest and vitality. The natural and simple dignity of the Bishop has been stressed, but he was also to the very end intensely human. People talked to him easily, and they felt not only his objective wisdom but his personal understanding and sympathy. The Bishop's whole life had prepared him for those interesting and helpful experiences.

He wrote:

> My belief is that the young and middle-aged who dread growing old, who stick to their jobs when they ought to retire, and who when they do retire soon sink into old age habits, have only themselves and their parents to thank for it. The years of youth and middle age are the years to prepare for a happy and useful old age. For instance, a man who has done a good job throughout life in business, as a clerk, a lawyer, a

salesman, who has brought up a family, finally decides to retire. He looks forward with dread to years of aimless existence. Of course he does, and he will begin to grow old fast, and perhaps become a care or a nuisance to his family and friends. Why? Because throughout life he has lived and worked on a narrow basis. The time comes when efficiency in the shop or office demands his retirement. Ten, twenty or thirty years ahead, and nothing to do. It is impossible. He won't retire, and he flounders on until he must; and then he quickly drops into old age, perhaps senility. Why? Because in his youth and middle age he has cultivated no avocation, none of the many interests which could give him days and years of pleasant activity.

It would be hardly correct to call the Bishop's interest in people an avocation. The problems were many times too serious for that. But he proved his own philosophy of retirement. His lifetime of service to others came into full fruition with his resignation. He had the happy asset when official duties were ended of being a guide and support to many.

Greatest of all, William Lawrence had the support of a strong and simple faith in God, a Heavenly Father as revealed in Christ. This came to him originally from the home in which he was reared, and he never tired of paying tribute to the influence of his mother and father. At the end of his life he referred again to the practice of religion in the home.

In these moving days customs change so quickly that it is very difficult for the people of even one decade to understand the habits, pleasures and interests of the decade before. This is the more true if we try to interpret the customs of a generation before. In telling you of the religious customs in which I was brought up, you would think it such an overdose of religion as to cause a sharp reaction and to make of me an atheist or a lost soul. I must emphasize this fact, that my Father and Mother were religious: they were happy, natural; they were not disciplinarians — no physical punishment — simply the leadership of two persons.

The whole family breakfasted by candlelight, for we had no gas, and of course electricity was unknown. On our way down to breakfast, we boys went into my father's dressing room for a short prayer. At breakfast he said grace. After breakfast, family prayers, the maids present, then off to school in Brookline, an almost two mile walk. On Sundays, again the two mile walk to Sunday School at quarter-past nine, service in church at half-past ten, including always Morning Prayer, Litany, Ante-Communion and sermon. Home to cold roast beef, baked potatoes, and cold apple pie. The cook went to church. In the afternoon my father drove us to the afternoon service while my mother read Sunday stories to the younger children. In the evening, family hymns.

This religious life and atmosphere was then as natural and interesting as are the motor rides, movies and games of Sunday afternoons today, with the result that faith in a Heavenly Father, in a loving Saviour, and the power of the Holy Spirit is a part of one's very make-up, which carry on through the doubts, the temptations, the intellectual radicalism and modern social life as naturally as the tree grown meets season after season of cold, hurricanes and glowing autumn.

The Bishop's religious life varied very little through the years from that beginning at home. Perhaps its very simplicity and naturalness give the answer. There was very little to be discarded in succeeding experiences. Yet it is interesting to realize the tremendous changes in thought which took place during William Lawrence's lifetime. Darwin's *Origin of Species* was published when he was nine years old. Thus during his span of years came the great development of science in every branch of human thinking and endeavor. It was inevitable that these great currents should affect theology and the interpretation of the Scriptures. It would not be correct to say that William Lawrence was untouched by these events. He was acutely aware of them and accepted them in large part as new revelations of the Truth of God. We must, I believe, go back to the simplicity and naturalness of the religious life of that Lawrence home in Longwood.

The Bishop expressed the fact in his words quoted above, written many decades later: "With the result that faith . . . is a part of one's very make-up which carries on through the doubts, the temptations, the intellectual radicalism and modern social life." This was true of his religious experience. It was just the opposite of the closed mind in the acceptance of a theological system. His religion was based upon a loving Father, who in Christ continues to lead us into all truth.

He never deviated from this point of view, from his days as a student at the Andover Theological Seminary to the brief address he gave in June, 1941, to the graduating class at the Episcopal Theological School. The Bishop was never a Jacob wrestling with God, or a Newman plunged at times into dark uncertainties and despair. His diary, kept faithfully every day, has not a single note of introspection. He writes continually of God's goodness, and of his own gratitude.

The Bishop was not and did not wish to be a theologian. Indeed, he had little interest in theological argument. His great venture in this field, his address entitled "Fifty Years,"[5] ran true to pattern, for it was a plea for the reasonable simplicity and naturalness of the Christian Faith. He was in no sense a mystic. There do not seem to have

[5] *Fifty Years* (Houghton Mifflin Co., 1923).

been hidden depths or heights. Certainly he was nothing of the professional ecclesiastic. Bombast, formalism, obscurantism were entirely alien to his point of view as to his life. He remained true in one sense to his New England Puritan background, for the simpler the service, the more the appeal to him, although he was tolerant of differing practices in this regard. There was, however, no note of Calvinism in his faith. Next to his home, he was influenced most by Phillips Brooks, whose gospel of the love of God fell like rain upon the parched earth of New England Calvinism. William Lawrence made the daily practical application of Phillips Brooks's gospel.

We are not all cast in the same mold. Some of us are more complex than others, and our religious needs must inevitably differ. Bishop Lawrence was in no sense a dogmatist in the contention that everyone must think and do as he did. In fact, freedom and growth were central in his entire point of view. He used to refer humorously to all the changes which had taken place in his lifetime. What was unheard of in his youth and early ministry was now considered as having been always. He knew what had stood for him the test of years.

In reality, there was a beautiful childlike character to his faith. By childlike is not meant childish, but the quality to which the Master referred when He said, "Except ye become as little children, ye shall not enter into the kingdom of heaven." This shone in the strength and the beauty of his face, and above all in the serenity with which he faced whatever life brought to him. Because he had faith, his life was happy.

II

The Family

IT MAY be true, as students of American life tell us, that large families are decreasing in number, and that the home does not occupy the central position as in other generations; but you cannot prove this general observation by the Lawrence family. The Bishop used to say, "So many grandchildren to date, but the phone may ring any minute to tell me of an increase in the number." He himself was one of seven children. Bishop and Mrs. Lawrence had eight children, one of whom died in infancy. At the close of 1940, the Bishop wrote in his diary, "Grandchildren and great-grandchildren multiplying. As I write this, one grandchild just being married. Children 7, Grandchildren 27, Great-grandchildren 5 – three more expected."

In 1933 he prepared a chart in his own hand of the descendants of his father and mother, and they total 170. In the corner of the diagram he wrote, "These records of ninety years of one family have been assembled and written by me with a grateful heart in my eighty-third year." Mr. R. W. G. Vail, the Librarian of the American Antiquarian Society, wrote him a letter of thanks: "As a piece of genealogical work, only a professional genealogist or a research librarian knows how many long hours you spent in gathering the material for this valuable record. Though it is possible that others might have made as good a showing in the record of their family history, I doubt if there are very many men of your age who could have written it out in such clear and legible fashion. Not a word is out of alignment and not a letter shows the least suspicion of a trembling hand."

The chart is remarkable for more than numbers and legibility, for here may be found the names of distinguished Bishops and clergy of the Episcopal Church, a Governor of Massachusetts, eminent surgeons, lawyers, and business men – leaders in their communities, all of them, men and women, who have shown the characteristics of high idealism and a great sense of responsibility. Here is an example of heredity at its best, all stemming from that Longwood home of which the Bishop wrote and spoke so many times.

The family meant a great deal to the Bishop. He literally with them lived in the past, the present and the future; and what a span he covered in his own personal association! His father, Amos Adams Lawrence, was born in 1814, only thirty-eight years after the Battle of Lexington. In 1941 Bishop Lawrence baptized a great-grandchild. If that child should live to be seventy-five, it would mean that the Bishop would have touched lives in his own family, starting with his father, covering over two hundred years. It was this fact among others which gave his voice such constant weight and authority, for he had been able to observe so much of the American scene.

In 1874, William Lawrence and Miss Julia Cunningham had been married by Phillips Brooks in Emmanuel Church,

Boston, for the new Trinity Church in Copley Square was then in process of construction. In 1924 they celebrated their fiftieth wedding anniversary in the presence of brothers and sisters, children and grandchildren, nephews and nieces, and many friends of the years. They had seven living children, five daughters and two sons: Appleton, then Rector of St. Stephen's Church in Lynn, and Frederic, Curate of All Saints' Church in Worcester. Through the fifty years there had been many experiences of happy service, in Lawrence, Cambridge, and Boston, interspersed with interesting trips to Europe, Egypt, and other parts of the United States. It was a happy, united family, and Bishop Lawrence gave as one of the reasons for his retirement his desire to be more with the family. In large measure this was the chief concern of his latter years.

The Lawrences had three homes: 122 Commonwealth Avenue, Boston, where they lived from November to early May; the Readville house, adjoining the estate of the Bishop's sister, Mrs. Hemenway, which they used for in-between seasons, September to November, and May through June; the Bar Harbor home, where they spent July and August. All of these were places for happy and constant family gatherings. Particularly was this true of Bar Harbor, which the Bishop had loved for many years, and where he had passed more than seventy summers. The family had four houses there, so that they were constantly together for picnics, sports, rides, church, and the Sunday evening hymn-singing which had been a custom for many years.

Bishop Lawrence had closed his *Memories of a Happy Life* [1] with the Bar Harbor scene:

[1] Page 424.

Our oldest daughter, Marian, with her husband, Harold Peabody, and daughter Gertrude live on Eagle Lake Road. Julia and Morton Fearey with their four boys, and Appleton and Hannah with their six boys and girls, talk to each other from their nearby piazzas. Ruth and Lansing Reed with their four girls, or Elsie from Portland, Oregon, with Lewis Mills and their two boys and two girls, or Sallie and her husband, Charles Slattery, and Fred come under our roof. On Sunday mornings we all fill half the transept of the church. In the afternoon at about five o'clock, after the majority have climbed a mountain or walked the Cadillac path, we all gather at our house and sing hymns until ginger ale and cookies appear, and then, after a little wrestle and by-play, the children call "Good night," and a quiet evening settles in. The full moon rises behind Schoodic across the Bay and casts its silver path from over Egg Rock Light to our open door.

The center of this happy family group was the home of Bishop and Mrs. Lawrence, and perhaps more Mrs. Lawrence than the Bishop, for he had many public interests and duties. She had helped most effectively in the duties which come to the wife of a Rector, a Dean, and a Bishop; but her chief interest had been in the family, the constant care of her husband, children, and grandchildren. No one can overestimate what she meant to the Bishop, her watchfulness over every detail of his life. Indeed, she in large measure made possible, by the smooth running of the household, and by the responsibilities she assumed, his great accomplishment in Church and public life.

Mrs. Lawrence, from the testimony of others and from her pictures, must have been a beautiful girl. As she grew older, she became a handsome woman, tall and stately, and while not old-fashioned in any way, possessed of a seriousness and quiet gentleness of manner which marked her as a truly great lady.

It was remarkable that in fifty-three years death had entered this large family circle only once in the loss of an infant daughter. But soon after his retirement the heaviest possible blow was to fall upon the Bishop. On July 4, 1927, the Lawrences left for Bar Harbor. Mrs. Lawrence had not been well for many weeks; even to friends who knew nothing of the facts, but who saw her walk by the house perceptibly more slowly each week and month, it was evident that there was something very serious the matter. The usual family gatherings and activity took place, but she passed an uncomfortable July, and early in August the doctor told the Bishop of the critical nature of her illness. On August ninth he wrote, "Best to say nothing to children at present. No advantage to them and J., and things may transpire better than I fear. I decline all invitations so as to have time free."

Both Bishop and Mrs. Lawrence were anxious to return to Readville. When the days and nights became cold, they had always been restless and anxious to leave. They both had a fear of being caught in Bar Harbor in the autumn by some serious illness; so they planned the return for August 29.

The night before, the Bishop wrote:

> P. M. About 40 in my study, children, parents, 12 maids from other cottages to see the movie films of our grandchildren, the Camp, Sand Beach, etc. Then hymns, and the last evening at Bar Harbor. Julia saw a few of them; the grandchildren came up to kiss her goodby as she cheerfully spoke to them — a breaking and touching sight to me. They little knew it was the last time. I think she suspected it. So closes our very happy life at Bar Harbor together for over forty years.

Mrs. Lawrence was greatly relieved to reach Readville, but there was no improvement in her condition, and it was clear that the end was not far off. The Bishop noted, "Dr. Frothingham thinks J. may live from one to three months. Wrote the children. Hate to write Elsie who is so far away." The time was not to be long, for on September 6 the end came peacefully, with all the family except Elsie present. After prayers read in the Readville home by Appleton and Fred, the funeral service was held at St. Paul's Cathedral on September 9. The Committal at Mount Auburn was conducted by the two sons, the Bishop with great difficulty pronouncing the Benediction. At the special request of the Bishop, at the service at the Cathedral all joined in the General Thanksgiving.

Gratitude had been one of the great characteristics of his life. As he often wrote and said, he had much for which to be thankful. It is good to see this same note of gratitude as he went through the valley of the shadow. After the funeral he wrote in his diary:

> Home at 1.15 with children and in-laws, 12 of us: a peaceful, happy family in their gratitude. Talked afterwards. Fred and Ap showed movie pictures of children at Bar Harbor and of my birthday last May 30 with Ma in it. Ap and his family left for Providence. Then Morton, in evening Julie left. So closed a day which I would have dreaded a while ago; though sad for us, sometimes overwhelming, yet her life so rich, it all seems almost natural in the course of normal life as indeed it is. Children playing croquet on the lawn. Telegrams and letters pour in with beautiful tributes and sincere sympathy.

At the end of the year, he closed the record:

> Closing of a year and of the happiest time of my life. Sense of loneliness tonight without Julia. I must go on with cheer.

Bishop Lawrence had a deep sense of reserve. It was at times difficult to realize the intensity of his feeling. Then would come some incident, and for a moment the curtain would be lifted. At a dinner given in connection with his eightieth birthday, reference was made to Mrs. Lawrence. The Bishop in responding broke for a moment and said, "I cannot read *Memories of a Happy Life* any more," and then went ahead with an amusing speech of reminiscence of those at the table. Never for a moment in the years to come was she out of his consciousness. At every anniversary or family event or reunion would be the note in the diary, "Missed Julia." He had met with serene faith and courage the great sorrow of his life.

Many elderly men are broken by retirement. They suddenly accept the fact that they are old and must act and think their age. Others find their mainspring gone with the loss of the companion of life. The adjustment to new ways of living becomes impossible. These dangers Bishop Lawrence surmounted. He had, to be sure, his family and friends, but deepest of all was his conviction that he and his loved ones were in the hands of God, a loving Father, who still had work for him to do. His direct and simple faith met the test of life and of death. Here was the source of his serenity, his amazing power of readjustment, and his will to keep on. How can this statement be made so confidently, for the Bishop did not bare easily his inmost feelings? Every year when Bishop Lawrence purchased his new memorandum book, he wrote on the fly-leaf, "Ezekiel 24:18. And at even my wife died; and I did in the morning as I was commanded."

That text was the keynote of his remaining years. At

once he took up life in varied interests and ways. The following week he went to Groton with his son Fred for a two-day conference of Church School Masters; then home via Providence, and tea with Appleton, who was now the Rector of Grace Church, Providence.

The Bishop wrote, "Lovely day. House seemed empty on coming home. No Julia to call to on entering, and none to welcome." But perhaps nothing shows better his indomitable spirit of youth than the entry a few weeks later: "Played nine holes of golf with Marian and Rebecca Hallowell. Beat them; tho I have not played for several years."

One of the concerns to which he set himself was the planning and the gift of suitable memorials to Mrs. Lawrence. There were two obvious places: Bar Harbor, the scene of such large and joyous family reunions; and Cambridge, where the Lawrences had been so happy when the large family of children were growing up.

On a perfect August weekday at Bar Harbor, a tablet in the Church of Our Saviour was dedicated in memory of Mrs. Lawrence, with the Bishop, Appleton, and Fred conducting the service and all the families and the children present. After the celebration of the Holy Communion, the Bishop read the dedication:

> To Thy Glory, O Heavenly Father, and in memory of Thy saint, Julia Lawrence, we dedicate this tablet. May the purity, humility and grace of her life be ours, and may our children's children ever reveal the radiance of her faith, hope and love, through Jesus Christ, our Lord.

The Bishop ends his diary that day with a note characteristic of him, "Just as Julia would have wished. Watched the children play croquet."

AT HIS MILTON HOME

1934

Later, very much the same family group, with close friends, gathered for a similar service in St. John's Memorial Chapel, Cambridge, when the new chancel was dedicated in the presence of the faculty and students of the Episcopal Theological School in memory of Mrs. Lawrence. The chancel had been previously greatly crowded. The Bishop described the change, "Everything inside has been torn away: clumsy furniture and pulpit removed; ampler feeling and richer altogether. A beautiful, simple service such as Julia would have liked: and how proud and gratified she would have been to have her two sons there!"

In February, 1928, Fred Lawrence made his father very happy by becoming engaged to Miss Katharine Wylie of Washington. In a sense, it meant another break, for Fred was the youngest of the family. As chaplain to the Episcopal students at Harvard, and more recently as rector of St. Peter's Church in Cambridge, he had been near enough to be in and out of the house for meals and for occasional nights. However, the Bishop's own married life had been so happy that he rejoiced when similar happiness came to his children, and he at once lost his heart to his new daughter-in-law, who was all he had desired for Fred.

The family gathered in Washington in the April of 1928 for the wedding in St. John's Church, at which the Bishop officiated. He had a wonderful time, staying with Mrs. George Cabot Lodge, the daughter-in-law of his intimate friend and classmate, Senator Lodge. He went sightseeing, visited the Tomb of the Unknown Soldier and the Supreme Court, and was pleased when the Chief Justice, William H. Taft, a friend of many years' standing, nodded to him from the Bench. He attended an ushers' luncheon and a family dinner, as full of life and interest as the youngest member of the family.

He particularly enjoyed taking the whole family to the Executive Office to meet President Coolidge. He spoke many times later of the occasion, and of the fact that the President never said a word; but perhaps it would have been more worthy of note if the President had spoken. One is reminded in this connection of the lady who remarked to the President in the course of a White House reception, "Mr. President, I am from Boston," to which the President is said to have replied, "Well, you never will get over it." Perhaps that is why, in the presence of the massed Lawrence family, the President did not break his accustomed practice of silence.

April 9–12. At Executive Office, White House. President received us as a family. I introduced them, and they passed by, he shaking hands with each and not saying a word: Harold, Marian, Gertrude, Julie and four boys, Lansing, Ruth, and four girls, Sallie and Charles, Ap., Hannah and three children, Freddie, Katharine, Polly and self: 26 in all, proud of the family.

After describing the wedding at St. John's, he wrote, and he could have said no more of his true feeling if he had written pages, "The climax of Julia's hopes."

The Bishop's life after Mrs. Lawrence's death continued much as usual, for he was determined to do "as he had been commanded." At one time he had considered making 122 Commonwealth Avenue, his Boston home, into apartments, but finally decided to keep the house as a family center. Miss Mary Cunningham, Mrs. Lawrence's niece, "Polly," came to live with him in the winter, an arrangement which brought great happiness to both of them. His daughters Mrs. Peabody and Mrs. Slattery were close at hand, and Fred across the river in Cambridge. Members of the New York families, especially his daughters Mrs. Fearey and Mrs. Reed, came often, and Mrs. Mills from Oregon at least once a year. There were grandchildren at Milton, Groton, and elsewhere. Appleton's family in Providence was only an hour away, so that there was a great deal of coming and going, in which the Bishop participated. He made frequent trips to Providence to preach for Appleton; he assisted Fred at St. Peter's, or sat in his congregation many Sundays; and he often went to New York for visits with the Reeds and the Feareys. When in New York, he enjoyed especially the dinners of the Round Table Club, where he took part in discussions of current events with President Nicholas Murray Butler, Mr. George W. Wickersham, Mr. Thomas Lamont, Judge Learned Hand, and others. He kept up with all his duties, such as those of the Harvard Corporation, but found time for constant touch with a wide circle of friends. He liked to have long conversations on the telephone with Miss Marguerite Kimball, for so many years his efficient secretary and devoted friend. He made frequent calls upon the sick in hospital and home. One of his friends suffered from tuberculosis; he had her constantly on his mind, and remarked continually on her courage and faith. Despite the necessity of readjustment and his sense of loneliness, he kept his life full and active.

Take it by and large, it would be difficult to find, considering the size of the family circle, a better-adjusted and more normal group of men, women, and children. It was, however, inevitable that there should arise family problems of health, education, and matrimony. To these family matters the Bishop gave constant and long-continued attention, consulting with members of the family and others outside who could give expert advice. He was never the dogmatist in these questions, but always the elder friend who tried to understand sympathetically the problems of another generation. He literally lived for his children and grandchildren.

When a grandson in boarding school was to speak in a competition, Bishop Lawrence wrote him a long letter of advice, "for I am a good example of how after hard work for years, one can have only very moderate success. I can at least tell you how not to do it." The letter is interesting, as it gives an insight into the Bishop's own methods of preparation and of speaking. First he emphasized his favorite theme, that a speech is simply a talk:

> "Make a speech" is a poor word. It starts one thinking of a crowd, a platform, a loud voice, etc. Hence, keep in mind when you are preparing your speech this idea. This is a talk to an intelligent listener: he is not going to answer back in conversation: he and a lot of others are going to listen to what I have to say, so I must get my thoughts into the best order possible, be clear in my own mind as to the movement of my thought, so that it will run off point by point without a great effort of memory, just as a pianist plays without notes, one phrase following another. I sometimes have my skeleton before me, but if I have prepared myself well, I forget that it is there, never look at it; and the speech is over before I realize that I am through. Don't cumber your memory with too much detail and exact form of language. If you have command of your subject and plan, the language will come.

The Bishop stressed the importance of posture. He always began his own addresses with a squaring of his shoulders, even in his ninety-second year. "Collect yourself with the thought, 'Am I standing firmly, easily, and naturally,' for if you are not firm on your feet, your audience will feel it and think that what you say is weak."

The letter concluded:

> Learn and listen to your own voice and so correct your faults: get others to correct, not merely elocution teachers, but anyone with intelligence and good sense. It is great fun to have once in a while an audience in the hollow of your hand.
>
> Good luck.
>
> Your affectionate Grandpa.

Then comes a final word, so characteristic of the Bishop: "P.S. Don't waste time in introduction. Move quickly into your subject and speech."

To another grandson in the Army, he wrote a letter of advice in August of 1941. It was four months before Pearl Harbor, and was written at a time when the international situation was so confused that there was considerable discontent among the soldiers, as they did not know for what they were preparing.

The Bishop began his letter.

> Democracy, thank God, is not made for war or for prestige in war. Hence, as compared with autocracies, Democracy is at immense disadvantage; it is unready and it takes time, strength, brains, money and patience to get ready; but given time, Democracy can beat autocracy in war, man for man; because a man educated in freedom has more intelligence, individualism, initiative and real fighting power than the man who through a life of military experience has been under orders, not obliged to think, has sharp limitations to his growth and power. Hence in the early part of a war the soldiers of a Democracy are liable to become critical, discontented and restless; to "pass the buck" on to the officers, the politicians and the general inefficiency.

The Bishop had seen this in his own experience in three wars. He continued:

What then is the soldier to do? I hesitate about expressing an opinion, for I am not a soldier, and am living a comfortable life. I should like to say this, however: the country for which our fathers fought and died, in which we have enjoyed freedom, home, and liberty, and which we hope to hand down to our children, is in danger. There is real danger that it be overwhelmed, and liberty wiped off the face of the earth. Every man, woman and child is bound to do his or her part; we have hardly begun yet, but we, all of us, have got to take our part. The soldier, strong, young, well fitted to stand up and fight, has his part; perhaps the hardest, especially now, when there is no fight. It is his privilege to lead in sustaining a spirit which will strengthen the whole country, and since he is sworn to do his part in Army and Navy, and will remain there for some time, he will be wise if he do *more* than his duty and gain such a reputation of soldierly spirit that he may be given more and more responsibility.

These letters are simply samples of many others. He followed children and grandchildren every step of the way, spiritually and materially. When the grandchildren reached the age of twenty-one, they received the benefit of a trust which had been arranged by the Bishop for them. He wrote to each an identical letter of congratulation, telling them the amount and source of the income to be theirs. On his birthday he always gave presents to children and grandchildren. He said that it was easier to remember the date of his birthday than to try to recall all of theirs.

After Mrs. Lawrence's death, the Bishop still continued the Bar Harbor life, making, as he felt she would wish, his home a meeting place for old and young, especially of the family. He was always available to them, except during the time of his afternoon nap. He did not wish the grandchildren to remember him as "an old man always lying down," and so up to the last summer he was downstairs at breakfast not later than a quarter past eight, and always read family prayers himself. The grandchildren knew in which drawer the special candy was kept, although they always waited for him to produce this himself. After breakfast and family prayers, someone would start up a lively tune on the piano, and grandfather and children would march singing around the table with vigor and delight.

When the Bishop was ninety-one years of age, he wrote a little article entitled, "A Modern Episode." It is reproduced here because it reveals his quiet humor, consideration of others, and youth.

In order to conserve his strength for the great day, Great-grandpa, after his morning bath, takes his breakfast in bed, reads half an hour, dresses and comes downstairs at half-past ten. This morning at nine-twenty, Generation Number Two comes over from the other house and asks if Great-grandfather will be on hand at quarter before ten to sit in a photograph of the four generations. Great-grandpa announces that he will do his best to be on the piazza, but could the photograph be taken five or ten minutes later? "The baby has her bath at ten," says Generation Number Two in a voice of finality. Great-grandpa immediately breaks off in the middle of an interesting article in the *Atlantic Monthly*, dresses, and is down on the piazza one minute before the time, and waits ten minutes for the baby, and the photograph of four generations is taken. Is that an instance of lack of consideration of the Great-grandfather? I do not think so. I think that it is testimony to the confidence of the younger generation in Great-grandfather's courtesy and vitality.

The Bishop took great delight in taking an active part in two moving-picture scenarios written by Fred and Katharine Lawrence. The first was a kidnapping mystery in which the Bishop was the father of the kidnapped boy and organized the pursuit, Appleton being the leader of the brigands. The second began with the Lawrence family in great affluence, the Bishop giving out shares of stock of the General Electric Company. When the plant of the Company is burned by the Communists, each member of the family, reduced to poverty, is forced to earn his or her living, Appleton running a Tom-Thumb golf course, Mrs. Slattery engaging in Prohibition propaganda, the Bishop acting as a fire-extinguisher salesman. The point of this role was that some time before he had actually been persuaded to buy some useless fire-extinguishers by a super-salesman – notably one of the few failures of the Bishop's remarkably keen business judgment. When other members of the family were skeptical about these devices, they were put to the test. A small fire was built on the driveway, but no one could conquer this feeble flame with the extinguishers. The scenario ends when the family is saved by Mrs. Reed's shares in the new Bar Harbor Club. The Bishop enjoyed all this family horse-play, and ran about as eagerly as the youngest, and acted with great spirit.

On Sundays the whole family always met in church, many times anywhere from twenty to thirty of them, and sat in the transept where had been placed the memorial tablet to Mrs. Lawrence. Then in the evening, after an active day, came the hymn singing, which always ended with "Mine eyes have seen the Glory," and then, all standing, "America."

So the months of July and August passed rapidly with walks, motor rides, and outside of the family intercourse with a wide group of friends. Of an older generation, the

Bishop had seen often Bishop Doane of Albany; Dr. Francis G. Peabody, so long the Plummer Professor of Christian Morals at Harvard; President Eliot; and Dr. Robert Abbe, the founder of the Museum at Bar Harbor in which the Bishop was greatly interested. Bishop Lawrence felt deeply the loss of these friends; but President Lowell, the Endicott Peabodys, Miss Eva D. Corey, Mrs. John Homans, the Samuel Drurys and many others were close at hand for calls or for luncheons.

To the very end, the Bishop kept in constant touch with his friends, especially enjoying luncheons of men, where the topics of the day would be discussed. Once he had planned one of these luncheons at his home. Less than a week before the date, he came down with an attack of pneumonia. Such were his recuperative powers, however, that he was able to come downstairs to greet his guests, and to stay for two courses. Mr. Eliot Wadsworth, active in the work of the American Red Cross, had just returned from Germany; and President Emeritus Angell of Yale, in connection with his new position with the National Broadcasting Company, had made a study of the educational use of the radio in a recent trip to England. The Bishop asked them to tell of their experiences. When the conversation started, he excused himself, and was asleep in his bed in not more than ten minutes. Such powers of recuperation are God-given, but the Bishop did his part by regular and careful living. He knew how many times he must travel up and down the long piazza of the Bar Harbor home to walk a mile; when he was not able to go out, he never failed in this exercise. But perhaps most conducive to health was his ability to relax, and his lifelong habit of not worrying. Gratitude, serenity, cheer — these were the three watchwords of his life.

Not all of Bishop Lawrence's summers at Bar Harbor were spent in family and social intercourse. He was deeply interested in the Church of Our Saviour, where, in addition to the Sunday services, he went to the Holy Communion on Thursdays, and where he preached once or twice a season, as well as in the other churches and chapels on the Island. He was active in the affairs of the Museum, and of the Village Improvement Society, and was particularly interested in the future protection and use of Mount Desert Island. To this he gave a great deal of time and attention, and had many friendly discussions with Mr. John D. Rockefeller, Jr., Mr. George Dorr, and others.

The Bishop expressed his feeling in this regard to Judge L. B. Deasey. It is an interesting letter, in that it reveals Bishop Lawrence's love of the past, and especially his dislike of the many and inevitable changes; but it also shows his realistic acceptance of facts, and is, as was true of all he said and did, forward-looking in his desire to see the needs of all the people met. He wrote,

> Since I came here over sixty years ago, and found only a fishing and farming village, a few boarding-houses, and three cottages just built in the Field, there have come changes and more changes. In those days the whole Island was ours to roam over. We climbed the pathless mountains, we had the summits of Green, Newport, and Sargent to ourselves, and felt the thrill of exploration. As to vehicles, we started with mountain wagons; then came buckboards, beach wagons, cut-unders, and, to our horror, some New York swells brought victorias and broughams. Almost twenty years ago the automobile entered. Meanwhile much of the charm of the old, narrow and winding roads has gone in the straightening, widening and

grading. Honestly I wanted no more changes; but as an old inhabitant, I felt that I ought to face the situation with an open mind.

He then made various suggestions as to possibilities in laying out roads, and concluded:

Frankly, I hate to write this letter. I turn my eyes from the scarred mountainsides which only time will heal. I dread the increasing multitudes of trippers; I shall miss the informal rough roads; I am weary of smooth surfaces and suburban-like surroundings. With this said, I am convinced against my own wishes that it is our duty as residents of this beautiful Island to make it as open as possible to the whole people. This is a National Park: it belongs to the Nation. Because we live here, we have no right to restrict its benefits. The people of the whole Nation, not only we, are supporting it: they have equal rights with us to its use. Millions will enter into the enjoyment of what thousands of us have hitherto delighted in.

The Bishop had no regard at any time for special privilege in Church, in State, even in Nature. He held that all were to be regarded only from the point of view of what was of benefit to all.

But to return to the Lawrence family. Bishop Lawrence had long been an interested spectator of the growth and influence of the so-called Group Movement, which had originated under the leadership of the Rev. Frank Buchman, a Lutheran clergyman who had been engaged in work among students at Pennsylvania State College until the Movement had spread to such an extent that he gave his full time to travelling about the world for conferences and personal interviews. The real reason for the Bishop's interest was the family, as Fred, Katharine, and Mrs. Slattery had been greatly influenced by the Group.

Except for this, it is fair to say that the Bishop under ordinary circumstances would have had little to do with the Movement, for his religious experience, as has been pointed out, was definitely normal and unsensational. It grew naturally and without undue incident. When he decided to go into the ministry there was no dramatic scene in any way. "One evening I told my father and mother, with whom I had never passed a word on the subject, that I hoped to be a minister. They were gratified; no doubt it had been an object in their hopes and prayers; and that was over."[2]

The Bishop's religion was as simple and as reserved as that. For himself anything more was unnecessary. He even looked somewhat askance at certain innovations in ordinary church practice. He wrote, "At Easter and Christmas we have today what did not happen twenty-two years ago: midnight Communions, sunrise services on the hills, missions, pageants, choir festivals – all well enough and sometimes stimulating; but when prayer and family hymns and the reading of the stories of Christian heroism are a part of the real life at home, they create a spirit, an atmosphere, and a character that are interwoven in life."[3]

With this background, there could be no appeal to him in the more dramatic methods of the Group. But he was intensely loyal to the members of his family in every relationship, because he had absolute confidence in their integrity of life and purpose, and he was sufficiently open-minded always to be ready for new indications of the moving Spirit of God. The Bishop, as always, was no auto-

[2] *Memories of a Happy Life*, p. 31.
[3] The unpublished paper quoted in Chapter I.

crat in Church or in family. He trusted, investigated, and tried patiently to understand and to share as far as he could the experiences of his children and grandchildren. Here is a good example for all parents, and this should be the true point of emphasis in Bishop Lawrence's relationship to the Group.

When he went abroad in 1928, he took the opportunity to learn as much as he could of Mr. Buchman's work. He had long talks with the Archbishop of Canterbury (Dr. Randall Davidson), and while in Oxford interviewed leading Dons and others. He held conversations with Mr. Buchman himself, the Bishop asking very frank and direct questions, emphasizing, in his own words, "my doubts as to the methods and manner of the Movement." To this Mr. Buchman replied, "Make criticisms and suggestions: we want this. Test us by knowing us. I hate publicity, and never answer false statements in public." He asked the Bishop to write and publish his mind and judgment on the matter.

This the Bishop never felt called upon to do. As has been said, his interest was personal, and he did not feel called upon to sit in judgment upon others. The nearest he came to a public opinion was a letter he sent to be read at a meeting of the Group in Boston. In this message, he recalled the various contacts he had made with the members of the Group in England and elsewhere.

"My observation, as I have said, has been to a good degree from a distance. I am not, and never have been, an insider, due to various causes. My life has been filled with other religious engagements. I am of an age when religious methods do not easily adjust themselves to new habits; and frankly, from what I have known of it personally, though not enough to enable me to be an unbiased critic, I have been somewhat bored and perhaps slightly shocked at some of its methods. With this said, I am a hearty supporter of those who gain spiritually by the exercise of its methods: and I know (and I say this with conviction) many men and women who, through its influence, have moved from lives of religious indifference to those of high devotion and saintly character.

"It becomes those of us, therefore, who are not intimately associated with the Movement, while careful of our criticism of that which we know but little – and that often at second hand – to give full appreciation and support to that which is good. May I suggest at the same time that the enthusiastic members of the Movement take note of the criticisms, and make sure that the Movement develops along healthy spiritual lines, as I know it has done to a good degree in these last years."

Bishop Lawrence's statement was entirely sincere and frank, but it was obviously very carefully worded, and was more guarded than would be the case in ordinary conversation. He could not understand the special appeal of the Movement for many reasons, but he welcomed the gift of the Spirit to other people; and above all he wished to share in so far as he could the experience of those of his children who at this time were members of the Group. That is why this episode belongs in a chapter devoted to the Bishop's relationship to the family.

Bishop Lawrence cared deeply and equally for every member of the family, but there was an especial bond between him and his sons. It was not simply that they were sons, but more deeply that the three of them had in common the opportunities, the responsibilities, the joys and sorrows inherent in the ministry. To him, it was like living his own life over again in their lives.

Fred Lawrence had become Rector of St. Peter's Church in Cambridge, on Massachusetts Avenue, just opposite the City Hall. The Bishop used to refer to himself laughingly as "Freddie's curate," for he was always ready to "fill in" when any emergency arose. When he was not officiating, he loved to attend church there, watching every detail of parochial life with affectionate, proud, and critical attention.

The Parish was composed of a large group of people, with a growing Church School and with a central location, but there was a very inadequate parish house, and the church itself was unprepossessing. The people were deeply interested, but not possessed of large means. Owing to Fred's leadership, and with great sacrifice on the part of the members of the Parish, and with the help of various generous donors outside of the Parish, an admirably planned and equipped parish house was built, much to the Bishop's satisfaction; but the modern parish house adjoining the church made that building seem all the more inadequate.

Mrs. William Caleb Loring, a sister of the Bishop, had left a bequest to be administered by three trustees – Bishop Lawrence, Appleton Lawrence, and Mrs. Frederic Cunningham, another sister. One of the purposes designated was a church building within the Diocese of Massachusetts. Accordingly, Bishop Lawrence wrote to the Bishop of the Diocese, asking for suggestions as to the use to which the fund should be put. Bishop Sherrill consulted with Bishop

Babcock, and both agreed that St. Peter's Church was the most strategic place under all circumstances for Mrs. Loring's gift, and so informed Bishop Lawrence. But he was fearful that the decision was made because Fred was the Rector, and wrote raising the question. The Bishops replied that the relationship was not the determining factor, and that they would take full responsibility for the choice. Mr. Charles Collens was chosen as architect, the contracts were let, and St. Peter's was made over into a beautiful church.

This whole matter gave the Bishop the greatest pleasure. He enjoyed building. When he had been Dean of the Episcopal Theological School, he had known every brick and stone. He conferred with the other Trustees, with Fred, with Mr. Collens; and it was a happy occasion when the church was presented by Bishop Lawrence to the Diocese; for here was not only an important step forward for the Diocese; here were associated with him the members of his family, and he was privileged to carry out the wishes of his sister.

The Bishop's relationship to Appleton was of course equally close, but Appleton in Providence was farther away. Bishop Lawrence, however, often went to Grace Church to preach on Sundays and in Lent, and always stopped off there on his return from his frequent visits to New York. As in the case of Fred, he watched with great interest and pride Appleton's administration of the very large and influential Parish of Grace Church in the center of Providence, and his growing influence in Diocesan and general Church affairs.

At one time Appleton had almost been elected Bishop of

Newark, but finally the Convention had become deadlocked. On October 20, 1936, however, Appleton was elected the third Bishop of the Diocese of Western Massachusetts. Bishop Lawrence wrote in his diary:

> Telegram from Springfield saying Appleton has been elected. Ap and Hannah came to tea at 5 P.M. from a funeral at Chestnut Hill: he had only heard that he was elected. Another telegram to them from the Transcript said that, although the Nominating Committee did not include him in their list, upon nomination from the floor he received on the first ballot only two less than a majority of clergy, and one less of laity for election: elected on second ballot. Very gratifying that he should have so far gained the confidence of Western Massachusetts. I had known that he was being considered, but took pains to hear and know as little as possible.

Appleton's election and acceptance were of the greatest interest and joy to Bishop Lawrence. Nothing just like this had ever happened before in the long history of the Protestant Episcopal Church. There had been numerous fathers and sons elected to the Episcopate, but extremely rarely within the lifetime of the father. Here was Appleton, elected Bishop of a Diocese which his father had established and for which he raised the endowment. The son would visit the same parishes to which the father had gone for confirmations over forty years before. To Bishop Lawrence it was living life over again, and he followed every step of the way with the keenest interest and delight.

The Consecration of the new Bishop was set for Wednesday, January 13, at Christ Church Cathedral, Springfield. The Bishop and Miss Cunningham motored down the day before. He examined with pleasure the new episcopal residence, and greeted the members of the family, who came in great numbers. The Bishop was eighty-six years of age, but no one was keener or livelier than he. Bishop Perry was the Presiding Bishop, and normally would have consecrated Appleton, but he had generously asked Bishop Lawrence to take that part of the service, in addition to preaching. The Bishop described the event:

> A beautiful day, bright sun, family breakfast with quiet family prayers, Ap reading Bible, I the prayers. At 10.15 he and I went down to Cathedral. Promptly at 11 the Processional entered the nave, not going out of doors; a packed, interested and devout congregation from the Diocese, Providence, and Boston. Jim Perry, Presiding Bishop, had courteously given me whatever of the service I wished. He took Ante-Communion and Communion. I took whole of Consecration myself. Co-consecrators Perry and Sherrill, Presenting Bishops Babcock and Moulton. Attending Presbyters, Freddie and Carmichael. Others, Bishops Cook, Dallas, Brewster, Budlong, Washburn. I preached the sermon, "Quickening of the Spirit." I dreaded singing Veni Creator; many years ago used to do it for Bishop Whipple; but my voice came out well: certainly my heart was in it; choir and congregation hearty responses; and the laying on of hands and whole service most moving — simple and dignified. "My Son," suggesting the unique features: no father having in history of church in this country ever consecrated his son: everyone seemed from what was said moved and deeply impressed; an undertone of joy and thanksgiving, and Ap is a worthy Bishop.

Those who were privileged to be present will never forget Bishop Lawrence. As usual, he was simple and dignified. He had a heightened color which belied his years: his figure was as straight as that of a young man, and his voice was as clear as a bell. As usual, he rose to a great occasion.

He began his sermon [4] by referring to the setting apart

[4] *The Church Militant*, February 1937.

of the new Diocese thirty-five years before, with a description of the work of Bishops Vinton and Davies. "As we now meet for the Consecration of your third Bishop, a representative of another generation, our look is forward, forward not only for another thirty-five years but towards a century fraught with such changes as will test the basis of civilization and the Christian Faith: for while the Diocese has been thriving like an infant in this little, happy corner of a country of wondrous prosperity and vitality, the world has been passing through a period marked by radical and revolutionary changes in philosophical thought and material, political and social structure. God has indeed 'put down the mighty from their seat, and has exalted them of low degree' in such a literal and startling way as to cause tremors to pass through us all as we lie awake in the night and talk throughout the day, 'and no man knoweth the end thereof.' "

He then described the development of material powers which had weakened the force of religion in the lives of so many people. He suggested the existence of a spiritual power in the great venture of Faith to be found in the service of Christ, and of what this would mean to the people of Western Massachusetts, every layman, woman, boy, girl, the mill worker, the farmer, the student and the professor, the shopkeeper, doctor, and lawyer. This would mean complete consecration of all, a new vision of the spiritual purpose of the Church (for the present hatred of the Church in Russia, Spain and elsewhere is a judgment on the Church for spiritual failure), and the courage to follow the Truth in fresh interpretations of Christian Faith.

The Bishop then spoke, as was so usual in the daily practice of his own life, of the power of gratitude. "I believe that the strongest and finest motive of a worthy life is that of gratitude to God, in the Name and Life of His Son Christ, for His goodness. 'A life of grateful service' was a favorite phrase of Phillips Brooks. 'Bless the Lord, O my soul, and forget not all His benefits,' is a happy morning song. Thus in the midst of heavy labor, distress, or confusion, the heart is calm, the life confident and serene; the undertone is one of joy."

At the close of the Consecration sermon, it is customary for the Bishop-elect to stand alone for a final personal charge from the preacher, who begins this conclusion with the words, "My Brother." Bishop Lawrence came to this point, Appleton stood, and then the Bishop, deeply moved, said, "My Son." These words more than any others emphasized the unusual character of the Consecration.

"My father used to say to me again and again, 'No man has ever been blessed throughout life as I have been.' And of all His blessings, this one stands high, that you are able to take up the refrain into your own life. With the confidence of the people of this Diocese, which will, I know, ripen into affection, you will go in and out among them carrying the gospel of a joyful, grateful service; singing to yourself 'Bless the Lord, O my soul, and all that is within me, Bless His Holy Name.' "

Following the service, there was a luncheon for some seven hundred people, at which Bishop Perry, Bishop Lawrence, and Appleton spoke. The Bishop ended the day with an entry in his diary:

Everything was most happy; a great day for everyone and especially for Ap, myself and all the loved ones. To me the only minor key was that Julia, who was the centre of all the years ago, should not have been there. At three Polly and I started for home: beautiful drive, sun setting, temperature of April. Nap of 2¼ hours until 8.15; quiet and grateful evening.

The Bishop's life was busy and happy, but, as was inevitable, there were sorrows and losses. Old friends passed off the scene, and he was called upon to officiate at many funerals. He had a way of concealing his true feeling. Many times, before such a service, in the robing room he would indulge in reminiscence in apparently the most light-hearted and off-hand way. But later his voice would break in the service when he came to the prayer he used so often, "O Lord, support us all the day long, until the shadows lengthen and the evening comes, and the busy world is hushed, and the fever of life is over, and our work is done."

In this period his sister, Mrs. Frederic Cunningham, died. She was very much like him in looks, in manner, in executive ability, in spiritual vision, and in her ideals of public service. Also, Judge William Caleb Loring, his brother-in law, for whom he had great respect and affection, died; and finally his son-in-law, Lansing Reed. Mr. Reed had married Ruth Lawrence, and they had a family of five daughters. He was one of the leading members of the New York Bar, a leader in many fields, especially among the alumni of Yale University and Phillips Andover Academy. He took cold at a Harvard-Yale football game, and pneumonia developed which could not be overcome. This came especially close to the Bishop, for he admired Lansing Reed greatly, and he felt deeply for his daughter and grandchildren. Although eighty-seven years of age, he went at once to New York for the last hard days, was a tower of courage and of strength, and officiated at the funeral at the Madison Avenue Presbyterian Church, with the pastor, Dr. George Buttrick, and Dr. Henry Sloane Coffin. Again he showed, and was able to impart to others, something of the serenity of his own faith.

The Bishop himself had a very serious illness when he was eighty-five years old, with an attack of the whooping cough. It sounds slight, but in a man of that age it can be very critical. He spent several weeks of great discomfort, due to paroxysms of coughing. The only mitigation was that he was delighted to be the oldest person of whom there was any record of having had such an attack, and he kept his sense of humor.

As the Diocese celebrated the anniversaries of his Consecration to the Episcopate, so the family marked especially his eightieth and ninetieth birthdays. He was born on May 30, and so was always at that season at the Readville house.

He marked the eightieth birthday by gifts to his children and grandchildren as well as to other relatives and friends. To some he sent his photograph, and to some twenty friends a silver paper knife with the date engraved. In the afternoon, a largely attended reception was held at the Readville home. The Bishop was especially pleased by the presence of Cardinal O'Connell. They had known each other, of course, for many years, and while never intimate had exchanged letters of congratulation and good wishes on the occasion of various anniversaries. The Cardinal's visit was appreciated as an act of great friendliness, and the two were photographed together in a picture which received wide publicity in the Boston press.

The great celebration, however, was reserved for Bishop

Lawrence's ninetieth birthday. Plans for this were made long in advance, the Bishop deciding that it would be both an afternoon and an evening affair. It was arranged that the afternoon would be given to a reception at Readville for nephews and nieces, even great-nephews and nieces, as well as for more distant relatives, near neighbors and friends. For the evening, a dinner was planned in the former cow-barn, more recently the badminton court, of Mrs. Hemenway, the Bishop's youngest sister, whose estate adjoined his. The dinner was limited to ninety of the direct descendants of the Bishop's father and mother.

All went successfully as planned. The family had at first feared that the schedule would be too much for a man of ninety, even though that man was William Lawrence. But he was determined to see it through completely, and actually was as young and enthusiastic in activity as anyone there. The youngest member of the family present was a grand-daughter four weeks old, who lay happily in the old family cradle, brought especially from Groton for this occasion. Some two hundred and fifty relatives and friends were greeted by the Bishop, who was here, there, and everywhere among old and young.

The toastmaster at the dinner was the Governor of Massachusetts, the Honorable Leverett Saltonstall, a great-nephew. Bishop Lawrence had been deeply interested in and gratified by his political career, had given a luncheon in his honor when he sought the nomination for Governor, and had helped in the campaign in every possible way. He was deeply moved when he offered the prayer at the Governor's two inaugurations, for personally it meant much to him that his father's great-grandson should be Governor of the Commonwealth; so that the choice of the Governor as toastmaster was most appropriate.

The place cards caused great amusement and some confusion, for many of those present failed to recognize their own photographs, which had been secretly secured. The Governor's was a picture taken at the age of three, the little boy somewhat unhappily astride a hobby horse. Just before the ice-cream, the big doors of the old hayloft, high up and across the length of the hall, opposite to the head table, rolled back, and about twenty-five of the younger nephews and nieces who had not originally been invited crowded into the opening and sang, "Happy Birthday to You," ending with "Three cheers for Uncle William!" There was a great cake with ninety candles. The young singers were invited to the floor for cake, ice-cream, and the speeches.

The Governor spoke, and read a letter of congratulation from President Roosevelt, whom Bishop Lawrence had confirmed at Groton School. Appleton read an original poem. Fred described the Bar Harbor movie, in which the Bishop had taken an active part; a few others spoke briefly, and the Bishop himself talked. Again he returned to the Longwood home, and read a description of that family life written by his sister, Mrs. Cunningham. He spoke, as he wrote in his diary, of "Grandpas Lawrence and Appleton, the number of descendants, including in-laws. My address was on the privilege of birth, wealth, and noblesse oblige."

It was a remarkable occasion and gathering, perhaps unique in American life, in the age of the Bishop, the number of the family, and the distinction in public service of the entire group, all united in bonds of happy affection.

The Bishop looked back to his father and mother. Mrs. Lawrence was of course in his mind and heart. There were present "a great cloud of witnesses," and before him in the younger generations was the long future of opportunity and responsibility. "Noblesse oblige," the keynote of his address, was the underlying note of his leadership and influence within the family.

III

The Diocese

DURING the first years of his retirement, Bishop Lawrence had little relationship to the Diocese as such. He preached from time to time, but he was taken up greatly with a trip abroad, his work on the Harvard Corporation, and many other interests. Bishop Slattery, who had come to the Diocese in 1922 as Bishop Coadjutor from the rectorship of Grace Church, New York, was sixty years of age, of great experience in Church affairs, and of tremendous energy. He had married Sarah Lawrence, a daughter of Bishop Lawrence, and they both threw themselves whole-heartedly into the life of the Diocese.

For some time Bishop Slattery's friends had been concerned about the strain he was beginning to show; but he characteristically laughed off any suggestion that he slow down. Despite these warnings, it was a great shock to all when, after a short illness, he died suddenly on March 12, 1930. In editorial expression, in hundreds of letters, in memorial services throughout the Diocese, deep sorrow was shown, as well as appreciation of Bishop Slattery's ministry. Bishop Lawrence, of course, was deeply concerned, especially for Mrs. Slattery, and was able to be a source of comfort and of strength in many ways, consulting with his daughter, and then making the necessary arrangements for the funeral service.

He wrote in his diary:

March 15. Continued expression of sorrow and affection in papers and everywhere. Chas. has impressed himself on the community, his ability and devotion have had cumulative force. Kept at telephone and details for funeral. March 16. At Sallie's, family met; Sturges and Freddie read Beatitudes and short prayer. 10.30, funeral service: Trinity Church, very beautiful and complete, masses of flowers. Students and clergy entered by Chopin's Funeral March; then nine Bishops, officiating clergy, and Standing Committee came down the aisle, Processional: we started up with them. Sentences by Bishop Perry. Church packed. Governor, Mayor, representatives of many bodies, delegates to Diocesan Convention and people. Fitts read Lesson. All congregation joined in hymn, Dallas read Creed and Collects. "O Master" sung on our knees. All Saints' Collect and Benediction by Babcock, and we went out in procession. To Mt. Auburn: Ap read Committal, I gave benediction. Altogether beautiful. A great testimony to affection and loyalty to Charles.

Mrs. Slattery met this great loss with high faith and courage. As the Lawrence family took part in the service there was the unforgettable impression of family unity and solidarity, and it was clearly evident on this, as on so many other occasions, that the Lawrences were both New Englanders in their reserve and Christians in their triumphant faith. With some people the phrase "altogether beautiful" in Bishop Lawrence's diary would seem an affectation; with him it was the natural expression of his belief in the Life Everlasting.

No matter what happens to individuals, the work of the Church must go on. Bishop Babcock, for many years the able Suffragan Bishop, with the Standing Committee, became Ecclesiastical Authority in charge of the Diocesan administration, and Bishop Atwood, retired Bishop of Arizona, and other Bishops, came to help with confirmations, for Bishop Slattery's engagements, made long in advance, had to be met. Bishop Lawrence was ready with advice, and held confirmation services every Sunday. However much he regretted the cause, it seemed good to him to be at the old familiar schedule again, and to visit once more many of the parishes of the Diocese. Everywhere he went, he brought assurance and strength.

In the Protestant Episcopal Church, a Bishop is not appointed but elected, for, contrary to popular opinion, the Church is thoroughly democratic in organization and practice. The various parishes and missions send elected lay representatives who, with the clergy, make up the Diocesan Convention. A Bishop to be elected must receive a majority of both clerical and lay votes, as well as later being approved by a majority both of the Bishops having a vote in the House of Bishops and of the Standing Committees of the various Dioceses. As we know very well in these days, democracy has its dangers as well as its advantages. It is an open secret that not always have elections to Church offices been conducted on the highest plane; and in the Church, unless we realize that democracy is at work and worth any risk, there has seemed an incongruity in the public discussion, in the press and elsewhere, of certain names as possibilities for the Episcopate. In this case there was, of course, as was proper, much quiet discussion, in which Bishop Lawrence took absolutely no part.

Finally, the election of Bishop Slattery's successor was

held in the Cathedral Church of St. Paul. Bishop Lawrence wrote the story of his part in the Convention.

May 8th. Having had no relations to the Diocese since I have retired, I did not go to the Diocesan Convention, but passed the delegates on their way into the Cathedral as I was on my way to the Harvard Corporation. At about 11.30 I received a telephone message from Dean Sturges that Sherrill had been elected, and that there was no other nomination, and that I was Chairman of a Committee to go to his house and announce to him the election. Although I have claimed not to be a member of the Convention, I could not withstand that, so excused myself from the Corporation, shot down the elevator and into a taxi, and arrived at Sherrill's door just as the Committee did. A telephone had preceded that a Committee was coming to announce his election.

We walked in, myself, then the Committee, Washburn, Sullivan, Sturges, Fitts, Judge Parker and Professor Beale. We found Sherrill, Barbara, his mother and brother in the study, all looking very serious, even frightened. I said, "Henry, I cannot say a word." He answered, "Neither can I."[1] So we shook hands and embraced: then I kissed Barbara: and the others were in the same emotional condition; for we were overwhelmed with the spirit of the Convention, and the heartiness of the election, of which Sturges told me as we were going up the Rectory steps.

We immediately jumped into a taxi, drove back to the Cathedral, and I jokingly said that Sherrill should treat us for the taxi ride; so Sherrill paid. We went in through the passageway, the Committee going into the front pews, Sherrill and I standing with Babcock. Only after a long pause to get hold of myself, I said, "Bless the Lord, O my soul, and all that is within me, bless His Holy Name. We bless God for the spirit of the Convention, and for the election of our dear friend, the Rev. Dr. Sherrill, whom in behalf of the Committee I present to the Convention."

[1] Bishop Mann remarked later at a dinner of the Episcopalian Club that this was the first time he had ever known either of these two gentlemen unable to speak.

Sherrill, much moved, said a few words of gratitude and of sense of responsibility, and accepted. Then Babcock added a few excellent words, and as usual inserted a little pleasant humor, which relieved the emotional strain of everyone. Indeed, Babcock handled himself beautifully during the two days of the Convention. Then I slipped out, and was back in the Corporation meeting downtown in half an hour from the time I left it.

It should be added that the Bishop, not expecting to attend the Convention, was dressed in a gray suit, turned-down collar, and rather bright tie. As he walked through the long corridor to reach the Cathedral chancel, he put his hand to his tie and with a twinkle in his eye said, "Not much of a costume for the occasion."

The Presiding Bishop formally appoints the officiants at the Service of the Consecration of a Bishop, but he customarily asks the Bishop-elect for his preference. In this case there could be only one choice for the preacher from the diocesan and personal viewpoint, and Bishop Lawrence preached and acted as co-consecrator at the service, which took place in Trinity Church, Boston, on October 14, which happened to be the thirty-ninth anniversary of the consecration of Bishop Brooks.

It is stimulating for younger preachers to realize the care with which the Bishop prepared such an address. On October 9 he records, "My consecration sermon so poor that I start on another."

October 10. Wrote all morning an almost new sermon for consecration: evening, finished up, wrote it practically three times: result, unsatisfactory but short.

October 11th. Evening, finished up sermon.

Oct. 14. I preached the sermon, and its directness and simplicity apparently had effect tho it did not seem possible.

The Bishop's later judgment was more accurate than his first, for the sermon [2] was deeply characteristic of his spiritual breadth and outlook. He began, "Men labor; they die; the institution which they served goes on. . . . A few years ago the Diocese met here, and with representative Bishops consecrated their chosen leader. In devoted service he gave freely of himself. His life and leadership entered into the Church, its Prayer Book, Missions, and its literature, and into the lives of thousands upon whom he laid hands in ordination and confirmation. God called him. The Diocese and Bishops again assemble, and in solemn service consecrate another, chosen to be their leader through the coming years; and the Church moves on."

The Bishop then described the great historic expansion of Christianity, with the observation that there is today a popular assumption that the Christian Church's progress has slowed up. This he denied, pointing out that "the last half century has witnessed a far greater activity of the Church in missionary fields than ever before, . . . that wherever the finest Christian faith has dwelt in the churches, they have like salt or leaven entered into the spirit, the traditions and customs of the people, gradually changing their point of view, lifting their ideals, and pouring forth fresh conceptions of life, public service, and self-government."

Bishop Lawrence was always practical and realistic, and next touched upon a favorite theme, the necessity that the Church should produce spiritual results. He declared that we in a country of settled traditions must beware of "pride in privilege and tradition, sogginess of enterprise, and an

[2] *The Church Militant*, November 1930.

indifference to the virtues for which the Christian Faith stands. And the very people who are building great fabrics and advertising their wealth of religious condition, beauty of music and ritual, who are content with numbers, figures, lofty towers and rich accessories, may be helpful in leading the Church towards spiritual decadence and bringing about its downfall.

"Great temples and beautiful cathedrals may be . . . an expression of local pride and denominational competition. They may lead to a fuller and richer sense of worship, or they may be a refuge to those who would escape the responsibilities of parish life. . . . A wealth of vital faith and an enormous amount of spiritual life, of civic justice, charity, and moral leadership must pour forth from our churches if we are to sustain our place and name as Christian."

The latter part of the sermon was an appeal for deep personal consecration to God in Christ in the fellowship of the Church. "My dear Brethren: we have assembled here as a family. You have asked me to say a helpful word to you, for I am your elder by several years, the oldest clergyman in canonical standing in the Diocese. Of those who take part in this Consecration, all, including the Presiding Bishop and the Bishop-elect, have been taught in classroom by me or during past years have worked with me. Upon a large proportion of you I have laid hands in confirmation. . . . I must now speak directly with deep conviction and love." The secret of the marvellous power of the Church may be found in history and in our personal experiences. "In Jesus Christ was and is Life. . . . What is clear to me, and I trust to you, that we want to make clear to the men and women and boys and girls about us is that consecration, full consecration to Christ on the part of anyone means an added force, a stronger personality in the community: one who has poise, charity, self-control, truth, justice, pity. When a man is really Christ's, all the forces of his life, intelligence, conscience, artistic sense, culture, athletics, gather into the centre, and consecrated by his Christ spirit make him the finer citizen, the more chivalrous saint."

The Bishop was fortunately incorrect on one statement in the sermon – "This is probably my last official address to you." As a matter of fact, he addressed the members of the Diocese once or twice annually for the next eleven years, and preached many sermons in the churches of the Diocese. So far as the latter were concerned, he did not in general like to promise that he would preach far in advance. He was subject to attacks of temperature which would keep him several days in bed, and he never liked to miss a public engagement, with the resulting concern about his health. He enjoyed particularly preaching in the churches with which he had special association, such as Grace Church, Lawrence, his first parish; St. Peter's, Cambridge, of which his son was the Rector; and St. Paul's Cathedral, which had been established in his Episcopate. He would make the arrangements perhaps only a few days before the Sunday in question, calling up Dean Sturges with, "Phil, how would you like to have me preach for you on Sunday?"

The Bishop in his preaching was, as in all things, himself; perfectly direct, simple and natural. If these three adjectives recur often in these pages, it is because they are

William Lawrence. He was completely removed from the preacher who is sometimes described in the press as a "pulpit orator." He seldom raised his voice, and was not given greatly to gestures. He was never impassioned, but gave the impression of sincerity and serenity. His topics and his illustrations were contemporaneous with the life of today, and his application was always practical and spiritual. He was a man of many affairs, but he was always the preacher of the Word of God. He kept clear of technical theological terms. He used to say that they should go out of use for a decade, they had become so stilted and shopworn. In reality, he *talked* in a quiet, personal way rather than preached in the popular conception of that much abused word, and he talked about those matters which were closest to his heart and mind at the time. As a result, there was a directness in effect which made a hearer feel that the Bishop was not addressing the world in general, but him in particular. Bishop Lawrence's ministry all along to the very end revealed increasing power as a preacher. Indeed, this constant growth and development were among the most noteworthy of his qualities.

Bishop Lawrence's attitude toward certain aspects of preaching was brought out in two articles he wrote, when almost eighty-eight years of age, for *The Church Militant*, the monthly paper of the Diocese of Massachusetts, to which he was a frequent contributor almost to the day of his death. Both articles were on "The Voice." Incidentally, the Bishop was peculiarly sensitive to people's voices. The harshness of modern voices was one of his few and most repeated criticisms of modern life. He wrote of a luncheon, "Sat between hostess and another lady, both deaf.

Others about the table shouted and screamed. Left when they rose from the table where we had sat for an hour, exhausted."

But to return to his articles in *The Church Militant*.[3] The first began with a description of the radio "as revealing the awful possibilities of the American voice." After a description of listening to the service on a raw Sunday morning when he was confined to the house, he continued:

And as to the sermon, let us leave the radio and go to church, for taking preachers as they go, they are more effective when one has the personality before one's eyes while listening to the voice. Not always, to be sure! The preacher may annoy us with certain mannerisms; he may be awkward in his movements, or never stand up straight, look only at the front row of pews, or up at a distant corner of the ceiling; yet whatever the limitations or distractions, we can see and feel that he is a sincere man, and that he wants to be helpful to his people. As a man and pastor, he is known to them, and what he is reinforces what he says, even though the substance of his sermon be obscure, dull, or impotent.

But the voice! And it is of the voice I am writing. Why, Oh why should a man who is cheerful all the week, who speaks to us pleasantly at ten o'clock in the morning as we meet him, strike a note of affected solemnity or anguish or perhaps shout as if noise were going to convert his hearers?

Turn on the radio to several stations just before twelve o'clock on a Sunday, or worse, at half-past eight on a Sunday evening, and before you have heard a whole sentence, you will know that a preacher and not a pleasant talker is on the air. Why, when a man preaches, should he strike a note different from that in which he talks? Why not talk on religion in the same voice in which he talks on art or the serious topics of the day?

One answer is this: when a man enters the pulpit, he unconsciously enters into a pulpit tradition. Stand a layman in the

[3] April, June 1938.

pulpit, and nine times out of ten he will have caught a preacher's tone and manner. I sometimes feel as if I would like to do away with every pulpit in the land, and let the preachers of the gospel begin again, and without the sermonic tradition, talk on religion as they talk in the homes of their people. . . . Laymen and women have no conception of the training and self-control that every young clergyman has or ought to have to escape affectation or conventionalities and remain simple and real in chancel and pulpit. And every clergyman who does his duty is from ordination to his death alert to continue natural and be his best self.

In the second article he continued his suggestions to the young clergyman:

Let him from time to time select one, two, or three intelligent members of his congregation to be his keen, sympathetic and constructive critics. Let him also occasionally place himself under the really skilled instructor in the use of the voice. This, I have to say, is a really difficult problem. The woods are full of men and women who call themselves "elocution teachers," "guides in vocal expression," "creators of orators and speakers," who turn out men and women of such affectations, mannerisms, and awful tones as make their listeners squirm and stop their ears. . . .

Let the clergyman realize that a congregation of one thousand is no different except in numbers from a congregation of one; and it is the one that he wants to talk to, simply and naturally; that quiet man in the rear — it is he whom the preacher intends to interest, to persuade, to move to a fuller life, in a natural, conversational voice in which he talks directly to that man, whose alert face responds to him from the very last pew in the church; it is he whom the preacher would gain for Christ. As he talks, he feels subconsciously the presence of the whole people; and as he reaches his last appeal, he suddenly discovers that beside that man, nine hundred and ninety-nine others have been listening, hearing, and also have responded. He who orates to a multitude touches no one: he who talks simply, directly, with the eloquence of a consecrated life to one man, moves a multitude.

The Bishop practiced this exposition to the letter. He preached as if he were talking to a friend in the study of the Commonwealth Avenue home.

The annual meetings of the Church Service League in January, and of the Diocesan Convention in the spring, gave the Bishop the opportunity to speak his mind on matters of Church and State. Reference will be made in a later chapter to his opinions on certain questions of national policy; here emphasis will be placed upon opinions touching the life of the Church.

Bishop Lawrence was a great believer in democracy in the Church. To him the laity were possessed of great responsibility as well as opportunity. In his Episcopate he had depended greatly upon the advice and help of lay men and women, for he was never the overbearing autocrat, but always the leader of clergy and people through the rightness of his judgment. He said many times that the great safeguard of the Church was the consecrated common sense of the great majority of the members of the Church. It was natural, therefore, that he should speak to the Convention upon the subject, "Honors and Responsibility of the Laity." [4]

He described the constitutional procedure of the Protestant Episcopal Church, in which lay representatives duly elected have equal power with Bishops and clergy, even in matters of faith and worship. He said that this placed on lay men and women the responsibility of leadership, and of great co-operation with the clergy, not only in matters of parish concern, but in the wider affairs of civic life.

"I know rectors, hard-working, self-sacrificing and be-

[4] *The Church Militant*, April 1937.

loved, who have high ideals of the influence and work of their parish and who are ready to do their part in leading in reforms of the community and bringing in a finer civic life. These men, working, calling and living among the people, see the awful results of gambling and drinking, of night clubs and immoral literature, of loose family life and disregard of the law; and they have in their parishes men and women, who, while regretting these things, do nothing to correct them.

"There are churches and charitable organizations in this State that are partly supported by the profits made in gambling and games of chance, and whose members insist that the law should not prohibit them. In so doing, they are undermining the habits and character of youth and undoing the very work for which they received their charters from the State. A few years ago, we were told that what society needed was not prohibition but careful license and an education of the young in moderate use of liquor. Prohibition has gone; but how many of the laymen and women of the Church, not to speak of the loud talkers *out* of the Church, are at work definitely in making our communities more temperate and more self-respecting? – How many are watching the work of the licensing commission – how many studying the effects of alcohol on our people's physique? . . .

"Is it too much to hope that, of the churches in this Diocese, every member of every Vestry be recognized as a man not only of good character, but of really high character who gives loyal support, not only in money but in his habit of worship on Sunday and in his life throughout the week? The pagans outside the churches are demanding, and rightly demanding, that the members of churches be distinguished for their character and public service; and if they are not, the pagans are ready to take their place and they will deserve to.

"For some years now I have been able to look at the Diocese in an unofficial way; and I am clear that when the laymen and women of the Church as a whole stand forth before their communities as of devoted, humble, true and self-sacrificing spirit and life, loyal to the Faith which they profess, the Church will have the confidence and support of the whole people."

Bishop Lawrence had lived to see unbelievable changes in the life of the American people. While he was youthful and forward-looking, he could not, with his background and standards, look with happiness at many of the fads and fashions of today. He discussed before the Church Service League [5] the changes in Church and personal life within the past sixty years – in the Church the development of parish houses, of better teaching, of more intelligent planning in the guidance of youth, of which he heartily approved; in personal life, the dangers "engendered by the freer habits of today."

"The force of habit was inculcated by the regularity of life. The adages of Benjamin Franklin as expressed through Poor Richard seem trite today, but they have much history, fact and truth behind them.

> Early to bed and early to rise
> Makes a man healthy, wealthy and wise

sounds almost ludicrous in these days of movies and motors,

[5] "Sixty Years," an address before the Church Service League, January 19, 1938; *Church Militant*, February 1938.

when night is turned into day, and day into night. The regularity of three meals at home contrasted with dashes into a cafeteria, the readiness to be off here, there, and anywhere, at the call of a companion, the easy breaking of an engagement to accept a pleasanter one, dissipate habits of life, overstimulate the nerve strings, weaken the force of a straight and firm aim in life. It is the unexpected that interests us, the disregard of conventionalities that tempts us. Youth with broken nights results in jittery middle age. The emotionalism of depression and recession, of speculation and uncertain gains and losses finds food to feed on in restless men and women. The deep tide of habit, quiet, self-controlled habit, gives strength, confidence and serenity, while upon the surface the incidents of the hour may harmlessly flash and play."

Bishop Lawrence continued with a discussion of the use of alcoholic drink. He was as far removed from the fanatic as white is from black. His conclusions in this regard were based upon his social conscience, his experience of many years with all kinds and conditions of people, and his sense of responsibility of personal example and leadership. Of course his stand did not meet with the approval of all, and it was entertaining to watch the expression of certain warm admirers of the Bishop change rapidly when he touched upon this topic which so affected their own manner of life. The Bishop had served wine at home until the war. Then he had stopped completely, and never again used or served liquor in any form. Outside of other reasons, the practical necessity and duty of efficiency weighed heavily on his mind.

He disliked greatly all the talk about the Eighteenth

Amendment. When that subject was brought up, as he put it, "I walk out." There is a popular opinion, even among certain clergymen, that it is impossible to hold a place adequately in certain circles without drinking. Bishop Lawrence was a living proof of the falsity of this point of view.

"Let us stop harking back to what might have been or has been, and take the situation as it now is. Let us be reasonable, and try to meet it with intelligence and patience. National, State, and local laws regulate the manufacture, traffic, and sale of alcoholic drink, and every citizen is bound to observe them. They leave the citizen large freedom, however, in his personal habits: he may never drink a drop, or he may drink himself to death, and be within the law. It is clear that beer is one thing, wine another thing, hard liquor another thing. It is clear also that the increase in the use of all of them is going on apace; that millions of dollars are spent in advertisement, and that in these times of depression, poverty and welfare aid, enormous sums of money are spent by our people in drink. . . . It is not for me to speak to other citizens, but I believe that it is the duty of every member of this Church to think out and determine what his duty is under the present conditions. . . .

"Forty and fifty years ago there were no such things as cocktails except in saloons and a few clubs. Today they are served throughout society before meals, between meals, at dances, and at cocktail parties. . . . I leave it to the physicians to tell of the effect of hard liquor upon the digestion of anyone, especially the young, even in small quantities.

"Others may tell of the effect of the cocktail habit upon the will power and the character. I leave it with any person of a fair spirit to say whether it is a fair thing to serve liquor so concocted as to make it impossible for an inexperienced young man or woman to know how strong it is; but this is where I bring my word to bear upon every member of this Church. What the Church has a right to ask of her members, every one of them, is thoughtful consideration and a decision as to his own way of life for the best of his own health and character; also how far he has a responsibility by his example for the welfare of others, especially those younger than himself."

The Bishop applied this general principle in a personal letter to a family of wealth who did a great deal of entertaining.

> I am sure that as you think it over, you will realize the responsibility that you take in entertaining young people, and you wish to give them entertainment which they will look back upon in future years with pleasure and not with regret. May I add that an experience of two generations in society has given me the opportunity to observe the decline in influence and leadership of those who entertain without restraint, and the rise in the respect and popular affection of those who, while entertaining beautifully, do so with restraint and an appreciation of the inexperience and weakness of their guests.

Bishop Lawrence returned to the theme of changing conditions in a later much-quoted address entitled, "I am Bewildered," [6] in which he discussed gambling, thrift, and Church Unity. In regard to the last, he was, as usual, eminently practical. He was always ready to co-operate to the fullest extent with members of other churches, and had been severely criticized by many within the Episcopal Church for his actions, but he had never taken much in-

[6] Address to the Diocesan Convention, *The Church Militant*, May 1938.

terest or part in the theoretical proposals for unity. What many considered a matter of debate, he had already done.

He began his address, "I am a somewhat bewildered man in these fast-moving days. I have lived a long life, and now so many things are discovered to be just the opposite of what they used to be, that I do not understand." He followed with various illustrations. "We used to be told that betting and gambling were economically unsound both for State and individual. . . . Now . . . we are told that certain forms of gambling and betting are not only harmless but really beneficent; so the old laws have been repealed, and, last Saturday at Suffolk Downs, half a million dollars changed hands. The Commonwealth is now richer and better able to support its institutions for the feeble-minded and insane. Indeed, the bigger the total, the richer will be the Commonwealth of Massachusetts! Why not boost the figure up to a million, or better to five million? No one except the losers will be the poorer: everyone will have had a good time; taxes will be lower, and the State enriched."

Again, thrift used to be regarded as a virtue: "Today we are told that the way to make money is to spend it before you get it. . . . Brainy men who have never earned five thousand a year tell us in a blithe and easy fashion how to borrow billions: it will all come out right in the end. . . .

"I used to be told that marriage was a sacred ordinance and of life-long duration: and now, why every eighth couple looks up with amused surprise and says, 'How old-fashioned you are! You don't keep up with the times.'

"I am a supporter of Church Unity, though I have more

interest in a unity of the spirit than of organization; and now I am told by certain earnest Churchmen that I must not allow a good Presbyterian to receive Communion at an altar of this Church until a visible unity has been completed. . . .

"Perhaps I have no perception of the value of rigidity; at all events I hope that I have some sense of humor and of right proportion. The fact is that I have been a member of this Church for over eighty years and have lived through many efforts to narrow its faith and standards; but its historic heritage holds it steady, strong, and broad in its interpretation."

The Bishop set for the habit of his own behavior gratitude to God that he was an American and a resolve to be patient. He told of Phillips Brooks's responding to a question as to his reason for being an optimist, "Because I am a Christian." The process of international understanding will take years, he said. He closed with a description of the deepest motive in his own life: "I chose the . . . adventure of faith: a will to think and act: a man: with complete confidence in God, my hand in His. Therein is power; a power that overcomes; a power that gives serenity and peace.

"It is that power which the youth of this country must have if we are to take our part in the happiness of the nations, in the coming of the Kingdom of God."

These addresses are obviously straight, practical, strong and clear. But it is difficult from the printed word to realize their effectiveness when delivered. There is needed the presence of the Bishop, with his clear enunciation and the serenity and strength of his expression and manner. He would come a few minutes before the time of his address in his familiar black cutaway coat and clerical vest, and receive an affectionate welcome from the members of the Diocese.

Usually at the Church Service League he would preface his address with informal remarks. Mrs. Richard Soule, a year and a half older than the Bishop, and the founder of the great Women's United Thank Offering of the Episcopal Church, generally sat in a front seat. The Bishop liked to greet her as "Ida," and recall the old school days in Longwood.

Then he would speak with utter directness and simplicity. Christianity to him was not a theory, but a way of daily living. Nor must we forget that these addresses touching the realities of life on a broad and modern front were given by a man in his eighth decade of life.

Bishop Lawrence had a deep interest in and an affection for the Cathedral Church of St. Paul, for one of the great accomplishments of his Episcopate had been with Dean Rousmaniere the founding of the Cathedral. He rejoiced in the central location and the simplicity of the church building, although he realized that certain improvements and enlargements should be made. At one time he had proposed these changes, but it was during the war, which made them impossible of achievement then. Dean Sturges was an intimate friend, and the Bishop visited the Cathedral often.

From time to time he enjoyed stimulating congregational singing at the Cathedral. It is an interesting picture — the youthful old Bishop in that particular role. A characteristic entry in his diary reads:

Evening: Cathedral, 7.15. Led congregation in singing three hymns, 159, 233 and 445. They had never heard 233, and I got them singing it in four minutes. Church packed. Standing in aisles. Carol service: excellent singing by choir. Preached.

The twenty-fifth anniversary of the establishment of the Cathedral was marked on November 3, 1937, with the same service used at the consecration, and with Bishop Lawrence as the preacher. Again he had lived long enough to see at the end of a quarter of a century the fruition of the original vision.

The Bishop in his address [7] described his and Dean Rousmaniere's plan, made possible by the gift of Miss Sophia Walker in 1904: the creation of a spiritual center in the heart of the Diocese and of the City of Boston, which would be literally a House of Prayer for all people. To him the essentials of the Cathedral had not to do with beautiful architecture, great towers, or glorious glass. The true essentials were the Chair of the Bishop, a representative organization, a central site, doors open to all the people; and above all an atmosphere within of sincerity, humility, and loyalty; a heart seeking the Saviour, and with the Sursum Corda rising heavenward. These objectives the Cathedral under Dean Rousmaniere and Dean Sturges had been achieved.

The Bishop then stated that "the people of these days justly demand from those who build great churches adequate spiritual results. The investing of millions of dollars

[7] "What the Cathedral Means to Me," *The Church Militant*, November 1937.

in Cathedrals lays upon the Church heavy, very heavy responsibilities. Is it not time to re-think the problem of the proportion of money invested in material construction as compared with the needs of money for spiritual purposes, the upbuilding of the whole people of this country and throughout the world in character through the knowledge and love of Christ?"

The Bishop raised three questions. "Do not the masses of people in our cities and throughout the country, most of them wage earners, many of them in want, look askance at the concentration of millions of dollars worth of material construction in a great and even a noble church? Second; Can or should the Church be burdened, in the light of the spiritual need, with such great debts? Third: What about the possibility of the taxation of churches?

"In view of these conditions, we come back with gratitude to our Cathedral Church of St. Paul. Like most loved and familiar things, there are features about it we should like to change; perhaps some of them may be changed as time goes on. We know, however, that in spirit and in fact it is a real Cathedral.

"The vista of opportunity during the coming twenty-five years will open as time goes on. The one great and stimulating service has been, is and always will be, in the gathering of all sorts and conditions of men in its daily worship. From its altar, when the seekers for truth, the disciples of Christ, the children of a loving Father have received of the very life of the Risen Saviour, they will go forth to the homes and parishes, to the cities and villages of the Diocese and beyond, to bring the glad tidings of the Gospel to a bewildered world."

Bishop Lawrence's last appearance at the Cathedral for a public address [8] was on the occasion of the Institution of the third Dean, the Rev. Edwin J. van Etten, September 30, 1940. The Bishop was then in his ninety-first year. Again he struck the same notes of democracy, service to all the people, and spiritual power. "I want to say this with all the force at my command; it has been a dominant motive in everything that I have had to do with the founding and support of this Cathedral.

"We of this Diocese happen to have the privilege and the responsibility of administering this Cathedral; we are Trustees – not simply for the people of our Church, but for the people of the whole community. If we fail in making this church a centre of spiritual refreshment for the whole people, for the Christian, the pagan, the outcast, the lonely worker, the intellectual unbeliever, the soldier, the sailor – everybody – we have failed at a vital point. Services should be so frequent, so varied, and of such spiritual quality that they will meet the needs of all sorts and conditions of men and women, of boys and girls. The services, the hymns and prayers will also sweep down the steps, across the street and on to the Common, as they have in the past, thank God."

The Diocese had always taken great satisfaction in the marking of Bishop Lawrence's various anniversaries as Bishop. On his tenth anniversary, he asked all who had been confirmed by him, or at least as many as could be admitted, to come to Trinity Church and re-dedicate their lives with him. For the twentieth, there was a great service at St. Paul's Cathedral, with the Bishop making the ad-

[8] *The Church Militant*, November 1940.

dress, and at a luncheon afterward the clergy and laity presented him with a beautiful desk which is now in the Bishop's office at the Diocesan House. In 1923, for the thirtieth anniversary, there was again a service at the Cathedral with Bishop Lawrence delivering his much debated and later published "Fifty Years." [9]

When the time for the celebration of the thirty-fifth anniversary arrived in 1928, the Bishop was not in the mood for a public service. He had retired, and Mrs. Lawrence had recently died, so at his request a service of the Holy Communion in Trinity Church was arranged, with only the Bishop, his two sons, and the Rector present. It was an unforgettable occasion – the great dark open spaces of the church, with the Bishop and his sons in the sanctuary, especially with the thought of the great throng present thirty-five years before.

The Bishop's diary for October 5 of that year reads:

> At desk 11.30. Boston, Trinity, at same place in chancel where I stood and knelt thirty-five years ago, I received Communion from my two sons! Sherrill, the Rector, the only other person in the church. I am the only living person who took part in my consecration. Happy thirty-five years, and everything to be grateful for, tho' depressed feelings possible as one thinks of the past, if one allows it; the happier way is to think of blessings, friends, and of those gone. Called on Henry Washburn, who has been ill. Sherrill had to meet me at luncheon: Cottie P., Billings, Sullivan, Slattery, Babcock, Sturges, Ap, Fred: nap at Sherrill's.

This group included a few of those closest to him, his sons, the Bishops, the Dean, Dr. Peabody and Mr. Billings of Groton, and Dr. Sullivan, Rector of Trinity Church, New-

[9] *Fifty Years* (Houghton Mifflin Co., 1923).

ton Center, long the editor of the Diocesan monthly.

When 1933 came, with the fortieth anniversary, the Diocese was not to be denied. At the Diocesan Convention a large committee of arrangements was appointed, with Dean Washburn as chairman. On the morning of October 5, the members of the Diocese, clerical and lay, met again at St. Paul's Cathedral for the service of the Holy Communion, with Bishop Lawrence as the preacher. In his brief address,[10] he recalled the day of his consecration.

"The Presiding Bishop at my consecration was Bishop Williams of Connecticut, who was born soon after the War of 1812, and only twenty-one years after the death of Bishop Seabury, the first Bishop of this American Church. The preacher was Bishop Whipple of Minnesota, 'the Apostle to the Indians,' of tall, spare figure, swarthy complexion, high cheekbones and long hair, who lacked only a blanket and feathers to be taken for an Indian." The Bishop concluded with a number of reasons for special gratitude to God for the blessings of the years.

In his diary he described the day as follows:

40th anniversary of my consecration. Henry Sherrill started preparations a year or more ago. Diocesan Convention appointed Henry Washburn Chairman of Committee. Many worked hard at it, especially Miss Kimball. 11 A.M. Cathedral by ticket, far more applications than church would hold. Choir in gallery. Processional. I went directly into pulpit. General Thanksgiving, then address by me. Celebrated Holy Communion. James Perry, Presiding Bishop, read Gospel: Babcock, Epistle: seven or eight Bishops. Church crowded. Great number of communicants. Very impressive service. Great congregational singing and Brahms' anthem. Lunch in the Crypt and parish rooms. About one thousand: jammed. Babcock

[10] *The Church Militant*, October 1933.

gave short address. William Lawrence Camp gave me a book of photos of camp. To Sallie's: nap. 4.30, Diocesan House. Tea to clergy and laity. Shook hands with many.

The great occasion of the anniversary was the evening in Symphony Hall. The hearts of those responsible sank when just before the hour of the meeting a very heavy rain set in, but the Hall was very largely filled with an audience of approximately two thousand people, a remarkable tribute in itself, and as a large part of the proceedings were broadcast, many more listened in.

The Bishop of the Diocese presided. Bishop Babcock gave the Invocation, and the Harvard University Choir sang. Addresses were given by Mr. William Fellowes Morgan, Secretary of the Church Pension Fund, and shortly to succeed Bishop Lawrence as President; Dr. Endicott Peabody, the Founder and Headmaster of Groton School; President Ellen Fitz Pendleton of Wellesley College; President A. Lawrence Lowell of Harvard University; and the Presiding Bishop, the Rt. Rev. James de Wolf Perry.[11]

It was on this occasion that President Lowell made his often-quoted tribute to the Bishop. "Bishop Lawrence has been right four and a half times out of five, and the other half occasion on which he may have been wrong I do not remember. He has had an uncanny faculty of being right; and, what is more remarkable, of not irritating people by being right. . . . What is the secret . . . of the wisdom he has ever shown? . . . It resides in the man himself, in his clearness of thought, his breadth of view, his disinterestedness, his attitude to life, to the many luminous threads

[11] Published in *A Harvest of Happy Years* (Houghton Mifflin Co., 1933).

woven into the texture of his character. He has been right so often because he has seen the present clearly in the light of the eternal."

All of these addresses were real, to the point, and effective. Many must have wondered what Bishop Lawrence could say. As he stepped forward, he received a great ovation, said a few words of appreciation, and then delivered perhaps his finest utterance, "An Increase in the Forces of the Spirit."

He began, "What weighs upon me, as I look back over forty years, is the increase in the recognition and power of the material forces." This has been due to the great advance in science. The result has been "to make men more ready than they used to be to accept passively what they feel to be the inevitable, to lay the blame on inescapable physical conditions, inheritance or nerves, and to neglect to call into action their will power, their finer ambitions, their spiritual resources: for to tell the truth they are not sure that there are such things as spiritual forces."

This attitude has been intensified since the war by the fact that economic competition has driven industry into mass production, in which individuality seems to count for little. Also we are weighted by "over-head charges," the "frozen assets" of a past generation, which need today new life. As empires and vested interests have passed away, because of a new spirit in the hearts of people, so the vital test of happiness in the Commonwealth is not in the form of government, but in the character of the people, in their spiritual temper and force. What is true of the State is equally true of the historic Church. When the Church has failed, it has been as the spiritual emphasis has lessened, and she has become gradually impregnated and then incrusted with pagan habits, materialistic ambitions, and vested interests, either in wealth, hierarchy, dogmas, or social tradition.

The Bishop then stated that his interest in the increase of the forces of the spirit, and more definitely the Spirit of Christ, had been at the base of his ideals and work in the Episcopate. His interest in the Church Pension Fund, higher education, the Cathedral, the missionary work of the Church, all had this purpose and goal.

The audience to this point had been held and were interested, but they were deeply moved as the Bishop gave what he termed his confession of Faith. He said that he came of religious stock, that as he grew older his beliefs had simplified:

"The Gospel of Jesus Christ, this Church of ours, its worship and sacraments, have been my continual stay: parents of deep personal religion, and a home where daily family prayer was as regular and as natural as the daily breakfast, have made religion and prayer a part of the texture of my life." He admitted that science had "made gashes" in his faith; but affirmed, as he had so often before, his choice: the venture of faith in a Heavenly Father, in His Son Jesus Christ, and in the comfort and guidance of the Holy Spirit.

He closed, "There is more, far more than this; experience, following Christ in daily life, companionship with God, prayer, brotherhood in the Church, are a part. But the real thing is that life has a meaning, an aim and a source of power untold. I know but little of this life, and less of the next life, but I know that my Heavenly Father is Love, Justice, and Truth. I believe that Jesus Christ lived that I might learn of him, follow him, pass through the gates of death with him. Why not? Other loved ones have gone before. Consecrated to him, fully consecrated, I find in him the supreme satisfaction, joy, and support of life. With this clear and final, what have I to fear from man, misfortune, disease, or sorrow? In perfect faith one may live on toward the setting of the sun, tranquil, and in perfect serenity."

With this moving peroration the meeting ended, except for the singing of "O God, our help in ages past," and the Benediction pronounced by Bishop Lawrence exactly on the hour. It pleased him greatly, for the sake of the radio audience, that every speaker used to the minute the allotted time and no more.

In connection with the anniversary, and especially because of his address, the Bishop received greetings from innumerable friends from all over the world – from President Roosevelt, Archbishop and Mrs. Davidson, Bishops, College Presidents, former students, members of the Diocese, and not the least welcomed, from the inmates of the Charlestown State Prison. His address made a deep and lasting impression. Mr. Thomas Nelson Perkins, a member of the Harvard Corporation, a man of great reserve, and not an Episcopalian, wrote him a letter which gives some idea of the general feeling:

I was so moved last night that when I got home, I sat down and wrote you a note. As one is apt to do when emotional, I slopped over, and so shall not send my note. But at the risk of seeming presumptuous, I do want to say that as you stood up there with all the vigor of a young man, and put into the atmosphere of the meeting a spiritual note which until you spoke I had missed, I was just as proud of you as if I had a right to be. If I try to say any more, I shall get involved. Perhaps if I have not given you any idea of what is really in my mind, you will take this as a word of very real affection.

The Bishop closed his diary for the day:

A great, successful meeting, and except for the storm a most successful day. Why all this should have been done for me I do not understand, for I know of nothing like it. Telegrams, letters, beautiful flowers. Henry S. referred touchingly to Julia and her help to me. A very, very gratifying day.

The Diocese had one further opportunity to express their admiration and affection for the Bishop on his forty-fifth anniversary in 1938. It would have been impossible to arrange another such day as that of five years before; so a reception was given by the Trustees and Faculty at the Episcopal Theological School, so close to the Bishop's heart. In the morning there was a celebration of the Holy Communion in the School Chapel, with the Bishop and his sons officiating, for the family and a few close friends.

The Bishop described the afternoon:

4–5.30, Reception by Trustees of the School to clergy and wives, officers of the Diocese and some of parishes: receiving line in Lawrence Hall: a steady stream for 1¾ hour — very friendly and informal — afternoon tea in the Library — talk and greetings on the lawn: 400–500 persons there and all seemed to enjoy it — a happy day.

On the occasion in 1934 of the One Hundred and Fiftieth Anniversary of the Founding of the Diocese, a Service of Thanksgiving was held in Symphony Hall.[12] Professor Joseph H. Beale of Harvard University described the early history, and Bishop Lawrence spoke of the past seventy-

[12] *The Church Militant*, May 1934.

five years. After speaking of the Episcopates of Bishops Eastburn, Paddock, and Brooks at length, he came to his own administration of the Diocese, with special mention of the division of the Diocese with the setting apart of the Diocese of Western Massachusetts, the establishment of a Department of Religious Education, the growth in the financial support of the missionary work of the Church, the founding of the Cathedral, and the Church Pension Fund.

What Bishop Lawrence could not describe was the large part that his leadership and character have played in the upbuilding of the present Diocese of Massachusetts. It is no disparagement of the heroic labors of earlier Bishops, notably Bishop Griswold, who had the whole of New England except Connecticut for his field, and Bishop Paddock, who painstakingly founded mission after mission, to state that the present position of the Episcopal Church in Massachusetts is due largely to two men, Phillips Brooks and William Lawrence. The background of Massachusetts is Puritan, and one of the reasons the Puritans came to New England was to escape Episcopacy. The situation was not helped in Revolutionary times by the fact that so many members of the Church of England were understandably enough Loyalists. Great credit must be given to Bishop Parker, then Rector of Trinity Church (and Mrs. Lawrence's great-grandfather), for his immediate action in removing from the Prayer Book the Prayer for the Royal Family. But the fact remains that many people for years were suspicious of Episcopacy. The situation was somewhat modified by the great influx of Church-of-England mill operatives at a later day. However, Bishop Eastburn was an Englishman by birth, and Bishop Paddock was not a New Englander. Then came Phillips Brooks, New England to the core. His election as Bishop gave a new connotation to Episcopacy. Bishop Lawrence followed, again of clear New England and Puritan ancestry, and was able to lead and to build for many years. He understood and spoke the language of the people. He combined hard, practical wisdom with spiritual vision. Whatever the Diocese achieves in the years to come will be due in large part to William Lawrence.

IV

The Citizen

THERE are many people of goodwill who will sponsor any number of causes, some of which may well be of uncertain value. Bishop Lawrence was not of this number. He believed in supporting movements for civic improvement or for the removal of injustice, but only after the most careful investigation and consideration. He realized that it was more effective to be heard occasionally on questions of great importance than to speak so often that people did not heed his voice. The result was that when the Bishop made a statement or took action as a citizen he was listened to by public officials and by the public, for they respected his long experience, his wisdom, and, above all, his disinterestedness.

One of the most striking of his public services was in connection with the Sacco-Vanzetti Case, which was rapidly approaching a climax at the time he was deciding to retire. It is unnecessary in this place to describe the details of this trial, which has been discussed pro and con throughout the world. Everyone is familiar with the story: two Italian Communists were tried over long years for the shooting of a watchman; there was involved the question of prejudice on the part of judge and of jury when the defendants were found guilty and sentenced to death. The verdict was appealed to the Supreme Court of the State, and finally to Governor Alvan T. Fuller.

It was at this point that a committee called upon Bishop Lawrence and asked for his assistance. Those making this request, among others, were Mr. John F. Moors, a citizen of high standing and a member of the Harvard Corporation, Dr. Morton Prince, the well-known psychiatrist, Professor Taussig, the distinguished Harvard economist, and Mr. William Thompson of the counsel for the defendants. The Bishop noted in his diary that they had come

> to ask me to gather a few men of high standing to urge the Governor to appoint a Commission to review carefully the case with a view as to whether he should commute execution to imprisonment for life. Case of world-wide interest. The Red Communist world everywhere feels that an injustice has been done in unfair trial, yet yesterday Supreme Court denied a new trial. But in my judgment a feeling among a great number of fair-minded men that doubt of guilt, that the trial not fair and that prejudice felt against them because they are Red. I said that I would give them an answer; feel that only just to urge and support Governor for consideration — a rather critical job.

Not only the men mentioned above urged the Bishop to take action; they were representative of a much larger number of people who were described in a letter to the Bishop as a "group that needs your powerful voice in order that the subsequent discussion of the case may be lifted to a more enlightened plane"; or, as another letter expressed it, "Thousands wish to rush our Commonwealth blindly into an act which should be based only upon calm, careful and fully informed deliberation. I can think of nothing more likely to make these people drop the mob spirit and do some honest thinking than the announcement that you were heading a Committee to approach the Governor about the case."

We may be certain that the Bishop gave the request of the Committee very careful thought. He was conservative in even appearing to intervene in such matters. Although deeply interested in prison reform and in the reform of prisoners, as far as is known he only once in his long career had signed a petition for clemency. He felt in general that our public servants could and must be trusted. At this time it would have been possible for him to have pleaded, as reasons for declining, his approaching retirement, the press of many affairs, and his age. But he felt in the present situation the responsibility of leadership and, though he knew it to be a "rather critical job," he consented to head a committee consisting of Professor Taussig, Heman M. Burr, Roland W. Boyden, and Charles P. Curtis, Jr. On April 12, 1927, the Bishop records:

Sent to Governor a letter saying that in Sacco-Vanzetti sentence thousands of citizens felt that they had not had a fair trial and asking the Governor to call leading and trusted men to his advice.

This letter, signed by the members of the Committee, stated:

Your Excellency:

Two men having been tried by the courts of Massachusetts for murder have now been sentenced to death. Confidence in the courts of Massachusetts which has justified itself for generations leads its citizens to assume that the sentence given is just and should be carried out.

There are, however, we believe, thousands of citizens of the

> Commonwealth who, having read or studied parts of the proceeding in the Superior Court as have appeared in the public press, have serious doubts as to whether those two men have had a fair trial.
>
> They were, as the law requires, tried by a judge and jury and found guilty. Motions for a new trial on grounds of newly discovered evidence were heard by the same judge and denied. Exceptions on points of law were taken to the Supreme Court and unanimously over-ruled. But the Supreme Court could not under our law reconsider and revise the findings of fact of the trial court of the exercise of the trial judge's discretion. Hence have arisen the doubts of the citizens for whom we venture to speak.
>
> Knowing well your sense of justice, your integrity of purpose, and your courage when assured of the rightness of your position, we ask with great earnestness that you call to your aid several citizens of well known character, experience, ability, and sense of justice to make a study of the trial and advise you. We believe that it is due to the exceptional conditions of the case, to yourself and to the state that these doubts be allayed and that it be made evident to all citizens that the Commonwealth has done full justice to herself as well as to these men, and also that you may have strong and intelligent support in whatever decision you may make.

At once there was a sharp divergence of opinion. Some were critical because they felt Sacco and Vanzetti guilty and objected to the Bishop and others interfering with the usual legal procedure. The *Boston Herald* had a leading editorial entitled "Bishop Lawrence Speaks" saying, "It is characteristically courageous and high minded of Bishop Lawrence to make the appeal to the Governor in behalf of Sacco and Vanzetti which has now been made public." Referring to the committee the editorial (April 19) stated:

> A group of men more distinguished in public-spirited leadership it would be difficult to find. Governor Fuller should take the advice of Bishop Lawrence. Let the Governor persuade a

group of men in whose conclusions everybody would repose trust to study the case in his behalf and as his agent. If, after talking with some of the witnesses and with the accused, these investigators concluded that the course of law has been correct, we should all be satisfied to see the sentences carried out. If these men found reasons for doubting the guilt of the accused, sufficient to merit an exercise of the pardoning power, they could in turn recommend that course to the Governor, and he would still be free to do as he pleased. That is all there is to it. It is a simple program, and one that has been greatly strengthened by the courageous action of Bishop Lawrence and his associates.

Similar expressions of approval came from many sources. A Congregational clergyman wrote,

> Your leadership at this time of prejudice is an additional cause for satisfaction to many men and women in all Communions, who have long found reasons to rejoice in your distinguished career as Bishop of Eastern Massachusetts. Not the least effect of your example will be the courage which it will give to young men in the ministry who are interested in the promotion of justice and in maintaining the integrity of our nation's political life.

On the other hand, there were those who were equally critical. A member of a college faculty declared that the Bishop's action had undermined faith in the courts: "I can only wish that in your closing days of a long life of service to the world you could recall your joint letter to the Governor and thus do something to help restore faith in our courts and in our highest Executive."

The Bishop was apparently unmoved by the clamor and conflict of opinion. He does not refer to the case again in his diary. He was too wise and too experienced in leadership to be too greatly concerned by the shifting tide of opinion. He had been asked by Mr. John F. Moors and others to perform a public service. This he had done to the best of his ability, feeling strongly the wisdom and the justice of the advice given Governor Fuller. That was all that he could do.

As is well known, Governor Fuller accepted the suggestion of Bishop Lawrence and his associates. Three advisers, President A. Lawrence Lowell of Harvard University, Judge Robert Grant, and President Samuel W. Stratton of the Massachusetts Institute of Technology were appointed. They made a study of the case and advised the Governor in effect not to interfere with the judgment of the court. Accordingly, the two men were executed at the Charlestown State Prison.

Bishop Lawrence on August 4 wrote Governor Fuller the following letter:

My dear Governor:

You will, I am sure, allow me to express to you my admiration of the way in which you have done your duty in the Sacco-Vanzetti case.

You have been wise, patient, dignified and courageous, worthy of the highest traditions of the Commonwealth.

At once many of those who had applauded the Bishop's first communication to the Governor became intensely critical, even vituperative. The Secretary of the New York Sacco-Vanzetti Committee telegraphed "Your congratulations to Governor Fuller on his death decree very unchristlike. But then Christ was never a Massachusetts Bishop."

No doubt the Bishop felt in this way about the situation: He had asked with others that the Governor appoint a committee of advisers. This the Governor did. Beyond question the Bishop had confidence in these advisers. Judge

Grant had been a friend from boyhood. President Lowell was a relative, and he and the Bishop had always been closely associated, especially in recent years in the administration of Harvard University. These advisers having reported, the Governor in connection with his own study of the case accepted their decision.

Again the Bishop could have remained silent. But feeling as he did, he publicly expressed his commendation of Governor Fuller with entire frankness and sincerity. Some years later a granddaughter while a student at Bennington College wrote a paper on the Sacco-Vanzetti case. The Bishop wrote for her benefit the story of his participation. He never regretted any action he had taken in this situation.

Bishop Lawrence in all his many public relationships followed his ideal of Christianity and of true Americanism, and these two ideals were linked closely in his thought and in his practice. He gave expression to this relationship in the lecture which he gave in 1929 at Milton Academy, where an alumni War Memorial Foundation had made such lectures possible. The Bishop was the sixth lecturer in a notable succession, and he greatly appreciated the opportunity of speaking and holding conferences with the boys of the school. He was always pleased with speedy and effective accomplishment. He noted:

> June 6 — 11:20 Milton Academy Chapel Memorial Service. Gave address and an hour's conference. Evening — Milton Academy gym. Gave War Memorial Lecture. Gym full and lecture seems to have been a success. In just a month from the time Mr. Field asked me the lecture was written, printed and bound.

For his address at Milton Academy Bishop Lawrence chose as his subject "The New American," [1] and stated that his purpose was to set forth "What sort of men and women [they are] to be who, from 1930 and on, will make up the American people, sustain and administer the Government, carry on the commerce and business, make and interpret the laws, preserve the health and weal of rich and poor, and so lead the whole society as to insure a happy and united Nation?"

Then the Bishop entered into a comprehensive if compressed survey of American history. He began with a characteristic passage: "Some people say that history is bunk; and others who do not say so may live as if they thought so. But the veriest modernist, radical, bolshevist, or flapper can no more get rid of his history than he can escape the fact that he had a grandmother. Grandma is still behind us, and she helped to make us what we are."

In this historical portion, from 1860 on Bishop Lawrence drew upon his own reminiscences. "My father used to talk to me of the soldiers of the Revolution just as your grandfather talks of the soldiers of the Civil War, and your father of the World War. While we were singing hymns in Saint Paul's Church, Brookline, I used to look around at Colonel Aspinwall, whose empty sleeve told the story that his arm was shot off in the War of 1812." He told of his father's sending guns to Kansas in boxes marked "New England Primers" and of the encampment of soldiers at Readville, of witnessing Colonel Shaw's negro regiment march up Beacon Street. He remembered his father's "say-

[1] *The New American* (Houghton Mifflin Co., 1929).

ing one evening, 'John Brown came into my office today and I told him to go to Whipple's to have his daguerreotype taken: he may be famous.' That portrait stood on our table for many years, long after John Brown's body lay a-mouldering in the grave and his soul went marching on." With this personalized history, the Bishop was able to hold the interest of his youthful audience as he came to the present.

Two conclusions were drawn, and they are prophetic of 1943. The New American will stand for liberty: liberty to live, to work, to worship, to learn, to write, and to speak. Secondly he will practice loyalty to Liberty under Law; Obedience to the will of the majority as expressed in the laws of the land is fundamental in the American way of life.

Bishop Lawrence then touched upon themes familiar to those who knew his point of view: the dangers of mass production and movements and of material growth without spiritual vision and responsibility and the resulting necessity of moral courage in standing for the right.

But also, he stated, there must be practiced consideration of others, and he illustrated this by his experience as Rector of Grace Church, Lawrence, where his congregation was made up largely of working people. This section is particularly interesting as revealing the Bishop's attitude toward labor. "There has been an enormous advance during these fifty years in the conditions, the intelligence and skill of the working people. I recall years when women and little children had long hours and unsanitary conditions: when it was assumed that the poor should keep their place and remain poor: when music, art, social life, and space for play were supposed to unfit them for their work. . . . Today the children of these people are riding in motors. . . . They have higher wages, more leisure, and better tastes." Then this significant statement: "The truth is that this advance has come to pass, not so much by the consideration of the stockholders, the employers, and the privileged, as by the determined struggle of the workers for their rights."

Bishop Lawrence expressed his own life-long practice of citizenship. "When the New American is faced with a question, whether financial, social, or political, he will come to his decision not merely on the grounds of what he wants, or what will be for his advantage, comfort, or pleasure, but what on the whole is right for the community and for himself as one of the community." This community is in essence larger than the nation, and again the Bishop was prophetic as to the responsibilities of today. "The essential thing is that each one of us, New Americans, realize that America, compact, gigantic and rich, shall by her character re-enforced by her power carry her share, even more than her share, of the world's load."

The Bishop closed with the characteristic emphasis upon happiness, serenity and faith. "Speaking for myself, I have not yet come across any science, or philosophy which has knocked out the faith in a Living God, a Heavenly Father, and the beauty and glory of His Son Jesus Christ: and the essence of this Faith is Love."

This address is a summary of the Bishop's own understanding and practice of citizenship. In scores of ways he showed his belief in Liberty and in Loyalty with consideration for all, for his life was given to a God "whose service is perfect freedom." The lecture afforded an interesting scene. The audience of boys to whom he was speaking averaged perhaps fifteen years of age; he himself was in his eightieth year. There was a cleavage of sixty-five years, but only theoretically, for Bishop Lawrence himself was perennial youth.

Bishop Lawrence was beyond question one of the most influential citizens of the Boston community – indeed of the Commonwealth. People of all kinds and conditions, representing all manner of causes, came to ask his advice and to enlist his support. Considering his age, and the fact that gradually he had withdrawn from all positions of administrative responsibility, it was remarkable that this was so. It made little difference whether he happened to be in Boston, in Readville, or in Bar Harbor, almost to the very hour of his death these calls continued.

The particular attraction which drew men to him was the unusual combination of high idealism and the plainest common sense, along with great experience and accomplishment. Although he had retired, he was never allowed to have the feeling that he was forgotten or left out. He never sat, as do so many old men, watching the world go by, because he was always in the vanguard of the procession. However, while always courteous and helpful, whoever the caller, he was careful to support only causes of proven purpose and worth. He never let his sympathy run away with his judgment. This made his support of a movement all the more influential. He was an infrequent letter writer to the press, or a signer of protests and petitions such as are without number in our day. He seldom appeared before legislative committees, though he was frequently

IN THE GARDEN AT MILTON

urged to do so. The result was that when he did speak, he was heard, if not always followed.

When the Bishop was eighty-five years of age, the Massachusetts Legislature enacted a so-called Teachers' Oath Law, which required that any person teaching in a Massachusetts educational institution, public or private, should be required to take an oath of allegiance to the United States. It was an attempt to combat so-called subversive teaching in our schools and colleges. But thousands of loyal and devoted teachers and professors objected, not because of unwillingness to pledge themselves to the Nation, but because they felt it unfair that they as a special group should be singled out for such legislative action. Furthermore, many of them felt that this might be the beginning of the suppression of academic freedom by the State, or to put it more bluntly, by politicians. There was bitter discussion throughout the State. When the bill was enacted, several influential professors resigned rather than submit to what was in essence class legislation.

Here was an issue which touched the Bishop in his understanding of the working of democracy. Key words with him had always been Freedom and Trust. This law cut across both his conviction and his experience. When an unsuccessful movement to repeal the law was initiated, he appeared before a joint committee of the Massachusetts House and Senate to advocate repeal of the law.

He began his address by describing his own life: "Born in Boston over eighty-five years ago, I have passed my whole life within the State of Massachusetts. For eight years I worked among the mill people of Lawrence, for nine years in Cambridge. For nine years more my field of duty as Bishop was throughout the whole State, from Williamstown to Provincetown, and for some thirty-five years in its eastern half. I ought therefore to know something of the character and temper of the people. Reared among descendants of Anglo-Saxons – for such was the population of Massachusetts in the fifties – I watched the incoming of the successive waves of peoples, the Irish, the Scandinavians, the Germans, the French Canadians, the Italians, and the other peoples of the Mediterranean Basin, of Russia and further East. I have noted that as each fresh wave has swept in, the settled population has been ruffled by a sense of distrust as to what might be the effect upon their own character, standards of living and traditions."

He then stated that as a result there were guarded attempts at repressive legislation, wise and unwise, but that gradually the new citizens, of differing background and traditions, had become a part of the population, which in a few years "was watching with some dread the coming of another wave with their strange customs." The reason for this assimilation is that "the atmosphere in the life here gives them assurance and confidence. My experience as a citizen of Massachusetts for eighty-five years is this: in the long run distrust leads to disintegration, confusion and then bondage. Mutual confidence leads to unity, strength and liberty."

He concluded, "Of all the great groups in this Commonwealth none is more worthy of trust than the group of teachers, from primary schools up and through the colleges. A legal restriction springing from a well-meaning and mistaken loyalty to our country is not fair to them, for it creates a consciousness that they are not trusted; and who of us can do his best work in an atmosphere of distrust? In these days of stress and uncertainty, we can conserve our liberties and traditions only by mutual trust and by confidence in the good sense, the high traditions and liberties of a commonweal. Hence I believe that the Teachers' Oath Law should be repealed."

The law was not repealed, but the Bishop had revealed his faith, not alone in the teaching profession, but in the basic soundness of American life. At various times in his public career he had been attacked, by those opposing his point of view, as a representative of the aristocratic and moneyed minority in the community. In reality nothing could have been further from the truth. He was of old New England stock, and was proud of that fact. He did have large means. He also had a reserve and a dignity which prevented undue familiarity. But as a result of his early training, and his long years in the ministry dealing with all kinds of people of every walk of life, he possessed a broad sympathy and human understanding. He had faith in democracy because he had faith in the worth, the character, the capabilities of the average man.

For many years Bishop Lawrence had been interested in prison reform, and for years had protested against conditions at the State's Prison in Charlestown. When the new Norfolk Colony Prison, with more healthful surroundings, with air and sunshine, and with improved methods of administration and of training was opened, no one followed the program with greater interest and with more enthusiasm. Once when there seemed to be danger that progress in this field would be halted, he spent hours in considering the situation, including conferences with Governor Allen and others.

He wrote of this new penology, "Do we citizens know that the Colony has a real schoolhouse in the center, and that, although there has been teaching, and often very good teaching in our jails and prisons, this is one of the first real schoolhouses such as to dignify the prison inmates ever erected in this country? Included in this movement are many facilities for exercising the men's hands, eyes and minds, giving skill to their actions, and preparing them to take their place in society when their sentence ends. After that, under the probation system they are guarded and encouraged in their jobs, or if unworthy, sent back for more preparation.

"If punishment alone is the motive of conviction and sentence, then the old-fashioned prison is the place. Let the worthless rot there; and for a prisoner of average ambition to make good, there is no worse punishment than to be thrown into his cell and compelled to do nothing. Of course he becomes stupid or restless or desperate, and ready, if chance comes, for a jail break or any form of excitement.

"But men convicted of crime are as varied in temperament, character and intelligence as other citizens. Some should be under discipline for life, others for many years, others for few years or months; but each and all are men, and call for careful study, sympathetic and firm individual leadership.

"If we are really an intelligent people, we will see that all who are convicted of crime have intelligent treatment, intelligent and well trained officials, and such stimulating leadership as will enable those who respond to take their place in society." [2]

These are the words of no aristocrat interested merely in his own class or group. They show Bishop Lawrence as he was, an enlightened citizen, and more than that, a lover of his fellow men, even "the least of these, my brethren."

Bishop Lawrence had long been interested in the very important matter of the control of venereal diseases. He had been a leader in attempting to secure better legislation on the subject. The war had increased his concern, and he had written a paper at that time upon "Venereal Diseases in the Army, Navy and Community." This paper was circulated widely and received much commendation from General Gorgas and others.

This problem remained in the Bishop's mind through the years. Toward the end of his life he again entered the lists, and gave an address at the Harvard Medical School entitled, "Social Infection and the Community." [3] For this occasion he prepared himself with great care, having conferences with Dr. George Bigelow, then Health Commissioner of the State of Massachusetts, and others. Of course it is a delicate and a difficult matter to discuss publicly, largely because so many people are unwilling to face the unpleasant facts. Perhaps nothing illustrates better Bishop Lawrence's forward-looking citizenship. He himself was an old man, as years go, born in the Victorian era when such questions were ignored in the name of high morality — an attitude not by any means out of date. He gave the

[2] "Common Sense," *The Church Militant*, March 1940.
[3] *Harvard Alumni Bulletin*, January 17, 1929.

address, as he stated, "not by preference, for the subject is not a pleasant one, but as a public duty."

With great frankness the Bishop sketched the plain facts of the prevalence of venereal disease affecting both the guilty and the innocent, and too often in times of peace hidden under a veneer of civilization. "First," he declared, "we must have facts, not social prejudices or traditions or expletives of horror, but facts. These are coming on apace through our modern social students and studies. There is no use in facts unless they get through the experts and doctors to the people. . . . In the past I have distrusted the advice of those who have pressed for common education in sex; but in spite of tradition, prejudice, and taste, I have been driven to the conclusion that the lid of silence must be wrenched off, and the subject treated in its fullness, as embodying facts of physical, social, moral, and spiritual truth."

The State and such private organizations as the Massachusetts Society of Social Hygiene are of great assistance in the program of education; but still much more needs to be done, especially in the field of the development of character. The Bishop asked, "In our break for personal liberty have we developed with equal rapidity the elements which make up what we call character, – a capacity really to use and rationally enjoy our freedom? Have we the self-control, the moral courage, the chivalry, and the unselfishness to be in command of ourselves and our liberty?

"In this study of venereal diseases and the infection of the community, I have been startled at the bare statistics, but I have been more deeply shocked and saddened by the revelation of loose living and immorality in this our American population. . . .

"This problem is not an isolated one. Like all human interests, it is bound up with the whole problem of man and life. The physical, social, moral and religious conditions are inextricably interwoven: every boy and girl, every man and woman is a unit, a most interesting, mysterious and priceless unit. If we are to serve this generation, doctors, social workers, and ministers must work together: parents, children, old and young must understand each other: whether the family live in a house, apartment, or basement; in a hovel or palace, the family is still a family, and upon mutual loyalties, loves, and sacrifices our health, happiness, and liberties depend."

These words were spoken several years ago, but are appropriate to the present, when with the coming of war our minds are necessarily focused once again upon this problem – no more menacing than in the days of peace, but more apparent. Bishop Lawrence, were he still with us, would be speaking the same message of honesty, courage and character.

The Bishop was from the beginning an enthusiastic supporter of the Greater Boston Community Fund. The union of the great majority of charities in one united appeal to the people of the community, with resulting budgetary advice and control in the elimination of waste and overlapping, appealed to his keen business sense. These campaigns were reminiscent of his own similar efforts for many causes, and he took great interest in the methods of promotion. He was called upon by successive Chairmen of the Fund for assistance and counsel. He enjoyed speaking over the radio for the cause, and at various meetings and luncheons. Especially he made an effort to speak annually at the Special Gifts dinner. He would appear just before the speaking commenced, and then close the occasion with one of his clear, simple, direct appeals. On one occasion the Victory dinner at the end of a successful campaign became almost a personal tribute to the Bishop.

The chief interest of the Bishop in the Community Fund went deeper, however, than business efficiency. He desired the more effective service of those in need, and he desired that this need be met by the sacrifice and the understanding of the people of the community. It is fair to say that at least in these days Bishop Lawrence would be classed as a conservative. He laid great emphasis upon the individual's sense of responsibility, and he was suspicious of the new development of governmental powers and services. He was fearful of the result in the weakening of individual initiative and responsibility. In an address at a Fund dinner [4] he said, "A great battle is being fought out in this country today between the armies of mass creation and of individuality; and in two years no one of us on either side will stand exactly where we do now. Between these two lines of battle is a broad No Man's land, and armies are marching forward, gaining a point, driven backward and forward.

"We, my friends, are on the battleline tonight. As never before the National Administration has moved into action in states, cities and villages, and sent supplies and support in the mass: and even though we recognize its dangers, we accept it in the emergency as a necessity. Forward come the citizens: 'Now we have the secret of national life: let

[4] December 6, 1934.

the Administration do it all. Why not? We pay taxes as heavy as they are. Why not add a bit, and get out from under the local burdens of welfare work? Let Franklin do it.'

"Why not? Because you and I, our friends and fellow citizens, cannot as men and women with brains, sympathies and ideals afford to do it. Are we ready to be mere tenders of machines, cogs in an industrial wheel? Or are we so determined to remain men and women, with tender hearts, with love of children, and of friendly spirit such as only personal touch can create? The national or city administration may supply the raw material: only men and women who know the hospitals, the Homes, the Helping Societies can supply the service. Each one of the objects to be supported by this emergency drive calls for services of medical and nursing skill, personal advice, wisdom, sympathy and patience which only men and women of heart and love can give; and thousands of such are pouring out life and glad service.

"We refuse to have a city of grouchy tax-payers supporting mechanically run institutions, though ever so perfectly equipped. We demand the privilege of helpful service, and we want a city of men and women of heart, of sympathy, and of joy which only the care of the crippled boy, the children in the hospital, and the glad sacrifice for others can give."

Here is found the real keynote of Bishop Lawrence's success as a money raiser. To be sure, he spent untold hours in securing the right publicity, in the arranging of lists, in the writing of letters in his own hand. But fundamental was his faith in the sense of responsibility of the average man and woman. He felt this for himself. He always in speaking to the workers told them, "Before you start to tell the story to others, think the story out for yourself, what you can give; and as Henry Higginson used to say, 'Cut into your hide.' Then, and not till then, can you have that confidence in the cause and in yourself which will enable you to ask for gifts from others. Do not be timid: do not be self-conscious or look for trouble. Naturally, and forgetful of self, ring the bell, walk in and talk as you would talk upon any subject that compelled you – cheerfully, hopefully, confidently; for remember that it is not you that have walked in and that talks, it is the great cause that you represent, the needs of a quarter of a million of men, women and little children: it is the City of Boston. Whatever your neighbors may or may not give, trust them, and assume that they have done the right thing. You do *your* duty, let them do theirs and therewith be content." [5]

These words give the secret of his own success in this field. He gave of his own means after careful consideration. He then forgot himself completely, and thought only of the cause he represented. Indeed he really felt that he was doing prospective donors a favor in giving them the opportunity to contribute. He possessed a unique objectivity. If anyone gave twenty-five cents, his response was, "Thank you very much"; if thousands or even millions were given, also, "Thank you very much." It was not to him but to the cause that the gift was made. To be presented with the opportunity of supporting those in need brought after all its own reward.

The last financial campaign upon which the Bishop en-

[5] Radio address, January 26, 1936.

tered was, as his campaigns went, for a comparatively small sum of money; but considering all the circumstances, no cause was more appealing.

The Rev. Dr. Endicott Peabody had undergone a serious operation at Phillips House of the Massachusetts General Hospital. There had been a long period of waiting and of anxiety. Mrs. Peabody had been disturbed to discover that amidst all the various buildings of the great hospital, there was no place where one could find quiet, strength, and peace in the presence of God. During these days she had felt the need of a chapel. She talked with the Chairman of the Board of Trustees, but the time was not propitious for the Trustees to undertake the raising of funds for any purpose, however laudable. Among others, she consulted Dr. Peabody's and her own intimate friend, William Lawrence.

He thought the matter over carefully, as was his practice. One day in high spirits he telephoned the Chairman of the Board: "I think that I should like to undertake the raising of fifty to sixty thousand dollars for a chapel at the M. G. H. It would be a fine way to celebrate my ninetieth year." Accordingly a definite proposal was made to the Trustees and accepted by them. Mr. Phillips Ketchum, a Trustee, became Treasurer of the M. G. H. Chapel Committee. Mrs. Francis Gray, wife of another Trustee, volunteered to assist the Bishop. The arrangement was made that whatever money was received would be turned over to the Board of Trustees, who would build and administer the Chapel.

Bishop Lawrence was like a war-horse who again scents the smoke of battle. At once he began preparing lists of possible donors, and especially arranging for the necessary printed material for the appeal. He always did this with the utmost care, writing and rewriting the copy, and being most particular as to the printing and even the type and color of the paper used.

He first called upon Dr. Richard C. Cabot, for many years a distinguished member of the Hospital Staff and creator of the Hospital Social Service work, now spread throughout the world. When Bishop Lawrence stated the purpose of his visit, Dr. Cabot exclaimed, "Splendid, Bishop, that is what I have longed for and hoped for for years! I'll give you five thousand dollars."

With this encouraging beginning, the Bishop began sending out the appeals, writing hundreds of letters in his own hand. As the money began to come in with enthusiastic replies, Bishop Lawrence was as happy as a boy. I doubt if any achievement of his ever gave him greater pleasure. He entitled the appeal, "My Postscript." He with the Trustees had given careful thought to the location of the Chapel, and it was finally placed in the very heart of the Hospital, as near to every branch of the Hospital as was possible. In order to obtain the proper atmosphere for the appeal, the Bishop visited the Hospital, and watched the constant stream of doctors, nurses, patients, relatives and friends.

Of course there are many Church hospitals with chapels, but it is unusual for a General Hospital to be so equipped. It is more than probable that this venture, made possible by Bishop Lawrence, will be copied throughout the country. Bishop Lawrence wrote,

> Through the corridors of the Massachusetts General Hospital some eighteen hundred physicians, house officers and resi-

dents, nurses, student nurses and paid employees pass each day and night, all intent upon the healing of men, women and children.

Throughout the Houses, Wards, and Out Patient Departments are sixteen hundred patients in beds, wheel chairs, walking with feeble steps or waiting for attention; in comfort or in pain, quiet or restless, anxious, homesick.

In reception rooms, in corridors, and patients' rooms are several hundred mothers, fathers, wives, husbands, sons and daughters, relatives or visiting friends, each and all with thoughts centering upon some one patient; perhaps four thousand souls all together.

Beneath the cheerful voices and small talk one can feel the deep tide of apprehension, sometimes of fear; now and again a wave of emotion sweeps over the surface; a bracing of the will; a heavy sigh, "Where in this great institution can I go for quiet?" "How can I escape from this talk?" "Where can I find refuge to sit and think?" "Where can I kneel down and pray?" "Where can I relax, confident that no one will disturb me until I have found myself and have gained my control?" "Where can I find spiritual refreshment?"

Where?

Here is the answer.

In the very centre of the great Hospital, along the main corridor, is a door that attracts and invites us. Passing through and shutting it tight, we are now outside the Hospital, which seems far, far away. We are standing in a small Chapel which is more than a Chapel, a place of spiritual refreshment. In beauty of architecture and warmth of color, in its atmosphere of repose and of peace, one feels a sense of rest and of confidence. It is intimate and friendly. No mortuary associations, no talk; but communion in higher realms as each one wills. Whoever will may enter here, of any creed or no creed. Yonder is a man sitting, then kneeling, stopping here on the way to his wife, while the surgeon is trying to save her life. Here is a young student nurse, who in preparing for her merciful calling is cut off from her village church and her parents' piety. Across is an agnostic who sits and thinks and thinks, and somehow gains courage to visit his sick boy. A mother and her son kneel close together, and feel the language of sympathetic touch. In a wheel chair is a frail woman, separated for weeks from her home and children. Sometimes a company of sympathetic faith joins in a short service; at other times the sound of organ, cello, violin, harp, or of a rich human voice. Faith is at hand, confidence, courage, hope.

Such was Bishop Lawrence's dream, a place, as he liked to speak of it, "of spiritual refreshment." It became a reality through the Bishop's leadership, and through the response of some one thousand friends of the Hospital, from every walk of life.

The Trustees' Committee engaged Mr. Henry R. Shepley as architect, and Mr. Charles Connick to make the stained glass windows. Bishop Lawrence left all decisions to the Committee, but attended many meetings and visited the Chapel frequently to watch the work of construction. When there were unavoidable delays, he pressed for action, for he desired to see the Chapel completed, and he was in his ninety-first year.

Finally, the builders were finished, the stained glass was installed, a small organ and a phonograph purchased. Bishop Lawrence had given considerable thought to the use of the Chapel, and at the suggestion of Dr. Nathaniel Faxon, Director of the Hospital, listed certain suggestions.

It must be kept in mind that this is a Hospital Chapel and not a Parish Church; that marriages and burials should be in the Church, not here. It must be borne in mind that there is danger of a tendency to drop from the finer, the spiritual note, to lower standards, jazz for music, light stories for better reading, a place to sit lazily and pass the time.

In our desire to help people, we are often tempted to be "uplifters," trying to improve, uplift or convert others. The purpose, however, of the Chapel and those who serve it will be to give all who visit it the conditions and opportunities whereby they will rise to their best selves.

To those who have the selection of the records or are responsible for the organ I would say, study the clientele of the Chapel, think out what will be helpful to them: some of the most unpromising in appearance may be the most appreciative of the finer music. On the other hand, keep in mind the simple folk. Think what it may be to some working woman from the general ward, anxious for her children, creeping in and kneeling, and from the silence comes the hymn, "Peace, perfect peace"; or another, as the glow fades from the windows, "Sun of my soul, Thou Saviour dear." The Chapel is not a music hall, but it is a place wherein music may have a beauty, a mystery, an influence which no music hall supplies.

And to those who select books my suggestions are but the echo of what I have said before. I have not the ability to select the right books, nor can any one person, nor can several persons at once and for all time. As the Chapel is not a reading room, the books will be suggestive, for inspiration, for comfort, for short relaxation; not of a sort as will tempt to a long reading. Study the people, ask your friends what has been of help to them, which books that you have selected are most used. They will run from deep, spiritual devotion to even short, captivating stories of chivalry, of victory over disaster.

There is not a person in the whole several thousand who walk the corridors of the Hospital every day who would not or could not catch a bit of fresh life, of faith, cheer, clear vision, and comfort, if he would overcome his bashfulness or feeling of strangeness, and slip into the Chapel for ever so brief a stay. It is for us all to make the Chapel a vital center, a help to healing of body and spirit.

These suggestions are deeply revealing of the Bishop's own character. They show again his understanding of people's hearts and minds, and his desire to be of spiritual help, free from fixed rules and regulations. Bishop Lawrence had been a great raiser of money, but it is fair to say that in every instance the motivating purpose was spiritual, a desire to serve the higher needs of men. This was true whether the appeal was made for education, for the Church, or in this case the Hospital Chapel.

Finally the Chapel was opened without any service whatsoever, it was just open; for it was deemed wise – a decision with which the Bishop was in complete agreement – that it was better, as it was to be used by all, that there should be no formal connection with any person or special group. There were even to be no memorials on the walls. The Chapel will stand simply through the years as "a place of spiritual refreshment."

The *Boston Herald* in an editorial entitled "The Bishop's Chapel," expressed the thought of the community.

> The good Bishop has done a number of larger and more notable things than this, but nothing more gracious, nothing more characteristic of his family and more worthy of its traditions. The list of donors indicates the respect in which the Bishop is held, as they include nurses, people in humble walks, well known residents of Boston and New York, and "President and Mrs. Franklin D. Roosevelt." Not bad for a man who is going on ninety-one!

The last public question on which Bishop Lawrence took issue was raised in the last years of his life as a result of an address made to the Annual Convention of the Diocese. Even after the passage of less than three years, it is difficult to recreate the atmosphere of April, 1940. Knowing what we do now, it is almost incredible that public opinion could have been so confused. There were those urging that we enter the war, others that at all costs we stay out. Feeling ran high, and names were called. The position of the Government had made possible the Lend-Lease Act. We were furnishing material supplies to the democracies abroad, but at the same moment we were selling scrap to Japan. It was at such a period that Bishop Lawrence gave his address, on April 10th, 1940.[6]

He began with the statement, "Every presidential candidate is claiming that if he is elected, he 'will keep this country out of war,' and those promises are cabled around the world. In return come back questions from correspondents . . . 'Why does not our country come in and help the Allies? Tell us, and let the world know.' "

The Bishop then repeated the familiar reasons: our hatred of war, our avoidance of European quarrels, our willingness to help by selling arms and munitions, the need that the United States keep strong to preserve the future of civilization, and to act as an adviser and mediator in the creation of a federation of countries.

He then followed with a much discussed paragraph. "Has it occurred to you that this statement of reasons, which we think sounds so plausible and sympathetic, is so smug and patronizing that if it sinks into the minds of the Allied peoples of Europe, they will scorn us as hypocrites? Of course the totalitarian states have no use anyway for our talk and boastings."

He recounted the sacrifices of the Allied Nations, and added, "Then they look across at this country, great and strong, talking so sympathetically of the cause of the Allies, and yet in the same breath, saying firmly that we will not enter the war, but that we will advise and may lead in the future." This country indulges in all kinds of luxuries, sports, amusements and extravagancies. We talk a great deal of international brotherhood, "but this Nation will not

[6] "Truth: Sympathy: Sacrifice," *The Church Militant*, April 1940.

risk a single life to join those who are defending the principles upon which our Nation is founded."

These are the qualities the Bishop named which the people of this Nation must cultivate: honesty, the frank facing of facts, intelligent sympathy with the conditions of others, and sacrifice.

"What I am trying to press home is that we put a softer pedal upon our talk of Europe, war and political and strategic guesses, and put a heavier emphasis upon the building of our own country in character and true leadership. . . .

"Let us rise, each of us, to the dignity of our work as father, mother, teacher, pastor, men and women who are trying so to live in the spirit of Christ that we have at heart the building of National character. We are far away from the realization of World Peace, but each one of us can do his bit in the creation of a manhood and womanhood, honest, sympathetic, and ready to sacrifice self for the good of others."

From our present vantage point of a post Pearl Harbor period, it is surprising to realize the furor which this address aroused. Even as the Bishop was speaking, the dissent of certain hearers was evident. There were editorials in the newspapers, and letters poured in of praise and disagreement. There were those who jumped to the conclusion that the Bishop was urging immediate intervention, and wrote in enthusiastic support; while others, reaching the same interpretation of his remarks, denounced him in violent terms as a warmonger who desired to place our young men in the front line trenches.

What did the Bishop mean? It is easy in reading the address to see in it a plea for our entrance into the war, but such was not Bishop Lawrence's purpose in that address.

The *Boston Herald*[7] printed an editorial with the heading, "What the Bishop Said":

> To understand either the letter or the spirit of the much discussed address of Bishop Lawrence before the Diocesan Convention, it is necessary to read carefully the entire text. The distinguished prelate has been misunderstood because only portions of that outspoken utterance have appeared in the newspapers.
>
> He did not declare for American intervention. He did define the qualities which we would be wise to cultivate as a people: honesty, determination to face the facts, intelligent sympathy with the condition of others, and readiness to adjust ourselves to others by mutual sacrifice.

That this interpretation of the *Boston Herald* is correct is shown by a letter of Bishop Lawrence to the columns of the paper: "May I thank you for your courtesy in interpreting in your editorial 'What the Bishop said.' " Furthermore, there was a letter in the Bishop's papers from a Chicago correspondent: "I am gratified to learn that you answer 'No' to my question, if you propose that our country shall again become involved in a European war."

Bishop Lawrence was clearly not urging intervention at that time. As a matter of fact, he felt strongly that such was not the function of the Church or of the ministry of the Church. What he was attempting to do was to clear the air of much of the hypocrisy and unreality of current thinking and speaking, and to recall the United States to her best self, that when decisions had to be faced, they would be made in sincerity and truth.

A year later the Bishop gave a more forthright address

[7] *Boston Herald*, April 20, 1940.

at the Convention of 1941.[8] Singularly enough, this address aroused very little, if any, comment, a fact which shows the great and rapid change in public opinion. This later address, despite all the developments in our national life since its delivery, is remarkably pertinent to conditions today. The Bishop felt the world situation more deeply than he allowed people to see. He was usually so serene and possessed, it is all the more revealing to find this note in his diary:

June 16, 1940. Listened to Kaltenborn, radio news reporter: a very vivid description of the terrific German assault, the end of France as we know her. I went back to desk to write, and for the first time since I left Julia's grave at Mount Auburn twelve years ago, I broke completely down. Polly tried to comfort me: Marian also: soon I quieted: put on my hat and walked on the lawn in the sun, and in an hour was myself again.

The Bishop in his address spoke of the last war. "It is now the fashion in some quarters to disparage our entrance into the World War. We are told that our young men had no business there and that we got our fingers burned in the fires of Britain and France. On the contrary, I believe that the idealism of our young men, the love of liberty, and the chivalry which sent them over to France, was one of the noblest deeds in our Nation's history. Their bodies lying in France and in this country are testimony to their heroism and love of liberty. The graves of the unknown soldiers are, by right, Meccas of grateful peoples."

He discussed with foresight the problems of a democracy at war. "The people in such a nation are bound to be unprepared for war in competition with a nation of mili-

[8] "Where Do I Stand?" *The Church Militant*, May 1941.

tary aggressors; that is their limitation and their glory. But although they are a people steeped in the arts of peace, they can, if given time – even though a short time – rise in military strength to great efficiency and power. . . .

"Now we are in a critical situation where every citizen must decide where he stands. Where do I stand?

"When we hear the shout from an impassioned citizen, 'I hate war, I love peace,' I answer, 'So do I.'

"Again he shouts, 'We must not send our young men to Europe to die.' I answer, 'What are you going to do about it if our first line of defense, Great Britain, breaks down?'

" 'The Germans can never reach us across the Atlantic Ocean.' My answer is, 'Men whose business it is to know, say they can. To the south or to the north, there may be lanes of passage.'

" 'We must have a negotiated peace.' 'Very good, but how are you going to negotiate with conquerors who have broken their word whenever it has met their convenience or necessity, and when it is too late to draw out?'

" 'It is against God's and Christ's law to kill, *Whoso shed's man's blood, by man shall his blood be shed.*' 'But what are you going to do if a bandit enters your house and starts to kill your wife and children?' "

It is evident that Bishop Lawrence saw clearly at that time the inevitable future before the Nation. There can be no question as to how he would stand today. What he would feel about post-war reconstruction is not so certain. Many of his warmest admirers had disagreed with his opposition to the League of Nations, a position he reiterated in 1941, saying that international peace stands before us as an ideal in the dim future. "The perpetual tragedy of the world is the high pressure in peace and through war to reach the immediate goal of a united world. Spiritual results take time; the mills of the gods grind slowly."

As has been said, Bishop Lawrence was a conservative, at least in so far as the present is concerned, though much less so than the great majority of his contemporaries. Considering the fact that he was born in 1850, and taking into account his background, the marvel is that he was so open-minded and progressive. However, he was cautious as regards world organization. As he put it himself, he was bewildered by many of the proposals and practices of the day. He stressed the responsibility of the individual, and the old emphasis upon personal initiative, and especially upon thrift. The expenditure of vast sums of money and the scheme of mass control under the name of social reform left him cold. He was no "left winger," no prophet of wide and instantaneous social reformation.

Who knows? Perhaps the pendulum will swing, and the personal characteristics which laid the foundation of our national life will once again come into vogue. This we may say truly, if everyone had the sense of responsibility and the love of his fellow men possessed by William Lawrence, there would be no need of reformation, for he was a great citizen.

V

Educational Interests

THE associations of an influential Bishop reach out far beyond the confines of the immediate duties and activities of the Diocese and of the Church. This was particularly true of Bishop Lawrence. In many directions, philanthropic and civic, he interested himself in various causes and enterprises; but it is fair to say that next to the Church he cared most deeply for the development of true education. He had respect for the great traditions of the profession of learning, and especially for the fearless search for the truth which was a central tenet of his religious faith. He realized the significance of the untold influence of educational institutions upon the future of the Nation and of civilization. But perhaps most of all, because he was always so youthful himself, he loved youth, and on the whole felt far more at home with boys and girls than with his contemporaries, whom he often found rather dull and boring.

At the time of his retirement, Bishop Lawrence retained the chairmanship of the Board of Trustees of St. Mark's and Groton schools and his membership on the Harvard Corporation. But shortly after, with the retirement of his friend, Dr. William Greenough Thayer, as Headmaster of

St. Mark's, and with the passing of the school into the safe hands of Dr. Francis Parkman as Headmaster, the Bishop resigned as president of the St. Mark's Trustees, carrying out his conviction that younger Trustees should carry on the School with the young Headmaster. Thus his relationship with St. Mark's hardly comes within the scope of this book.

Bishop Lawrence's connection with Groton was unique. For fifty-six years up to 1940, from the very beginning of the School, he was a Trustee, for nine of these years he served as Secretary, and for forty-seven years as President of the Board. During this period he watched with helpful interest the development of the School under the leadership of Dr. Endicott Peabody, from a large number of acres of farm land to the great school of today, with all of its traditions and achievements. During these years Bishop Lawrence had been a constant and wise advisor. But the relationship went deeper than that of the average trustee to an institution. Dr. and Mrs. Peabody were among the Bishop's oldest and dearest friends – "Cottie and Fannie," as he referred to them. Their home, particularly after Mrs. Lawrence's death, was a haven of comfort, and if not of peace, at least of absorbing interest and activity. He made various attempts to resign his Presidency, but was always persuaded to stay on until Dr. Peabody retired; and this he did. Groton was the one place where he went annually for a confirmation visitation. Beyond question, he confirmed the great majority of the graduates of the School, including the present President of the United States.

It cannot be said that the problems of the School were greatly complicated during this latter part of Bishop Lawrence's life, but he took the deepest interest in every detail, presided at the meetings of the Board, attended the more frequent meetings of the Standing Committee, which often met at his house, and was always ready to consult on questions large and small with the Rector.

The two great events in this period for Bishop Lawrence were the celebration of the School's Fiftieth Anniversary, and the Farewell to Dr. Peabody as Headmaster. On both of these occasions Bishop Lawrence took a full and active part.

The Fiftieth Anniversary was celebrated in the first week of June, 1934, with President Franklin D. Roosevelt in attendance. Bishop Lawrence described the celebration in his diary.

June 1. Polly drove me up to Groton Prize Day; also beginning 50th Anniversary celebration of the School. Lovely day. Pres. Roosevelt and suite came on grounds as we did. Service in the Chapel. To the Hall of School House: large company there this year: too many to get in. Cottie opened the exercises with his report: then introduced Lawrence Lowell, Speaker of the day. Then I spoke on the value to the work and life of the School of the Undermasters, illustrated by Amory Gardner and Billings.[1] The President sat with his wife and family, not on the platform. Fannie gave the prizes, and Cottie the diplomas: each boy shook the President's hand as they came down. John R., his son, graduated. To lunch in 100 House, big crowd: buffet lunch except a dozen at the high table: Fannie, President, etc. at one end: Mrs. Roosevelt at other end, Lawrence L. at her left, I on her right, Mrs. R., the President's mother, on my right.

Evening: Went to buffet supper at the Hunt Club: about 150 graduates there. In behalf of Trustees I presented to Cottie

[1] William Amory Gardner and the Rev. Sherrard Billings, original associates of Dr. Peabody in founding the School.

and Fannie each a block of silver engraved with Groton coat of arms, and for 50 years' service. Then to my great surprise Redmond Cross presented me with the same. I spoke about Cottie's Father, and what he was to the School in its early days. 3 or 4 excellent short speeches: then choir, and everyone present joined in Groton singsong. Very successful evening.

Saturday, June 2. Very hot day: to the School. Baseball, other games and loafing. Pres. and Mrs. R. around like the rest. P.M.: Took it easy. Others at boatrace on the river: tea at the School, lots of friends, old boys, etc. 7 P.M.: Great dinner in 100 House, 600 plates. I sat between Fannie and Frank Polk. Pres. at table with his own form. Gordon Bell was toastmaster. Frank Ashburn spoke: then I did on "Three Grotonians," George Rublee, Cottie and Pres. Roosevelt. I spoke direct to the President, told him what Groton thought of him, of course not always agreeing with his policies, but with the greatest admiration for himself, his character, courage, etc. He looked straight at me from the beginning to end, and I apparently struck the right note. The President said that he was trying to make Nation play the game and hold to the rules. A fine dinner, all agreed.

Sunday, June 3. Service in Chapel. Cottie preached. In chancel with him, myself, and the alumni (in the ministry), Malcolm, Crocker, Sturges and Zabriskie.[2] After lunch the company broke up. All agreed it a most successful celebration.

The second important event in Groton's history during these years was Dr. Peabody's resignation in June of 1940.[3] On Prize Day Bishop Lawrence spoke among others testifying to the life and influence of Endicott Peabody.

"For fifty-six years we have been together as trustees, more years than that as friends, and in those earlier years

[2] Dr. Peabody's son, Malcolm, Bishop of Central New York; the Rev. John Crocker, Headmaster of Groton; the Rev. Philemon Sturges, Rector of St. Andrew's, Wellesley; Dean Alexander Zabriskie, of the Virginia Seminary.

[3] *Groton School Quarterly*, June 1940.

he told me of his expectation of founding the school. And now for fifty-six years we have been together, and I shall say nothing about him more than this – that of all the fifty-six Prize Day speeches he has made, that of this year was lighter and more humorous than the one before, and the one before was more humorous than the preceding one. In other words, as the years have gone on, the Rector has mellowed. There were Prize Days only a few years ago when parents shrank from coming to the exercises, because the Rector felt, as he told me himself, 'It is the only time I can get hold of the parents, and I give it to them!' But with the kindness of Mrs. Peabody and the warnings of some of his friends there grew into his soul a richness of temper and a vein of humor which made him what he is, and if he went on improving, the time would come when there would really be nothing strong or rigid left in him!"

The Bishop then in serious vein read a letter coming from the Board of Trustees, but in reality composed entirely by himself. This letter was described by Bishop Lawrence as one "of reminiscence and of record." In it he told of the founding and the growth of the School, and stated that this had come about through the character, personality and leadership of Dr. Peabody.

"Fifty-six years ago Groton School's plant was a single building on a farm lying on a beautiful slope to the Nashua River, with Wachusett and Monadnock across the valley – a scene now bound up in the affection of graduates scattered all over the world. Today the School has the same beautiful outlook; a Chapel whose chimes, rung by the boys, sound across the valley; many buildings; and a most generous endowment. These all betoken confidence in you. Indeed, I believe that the exaltation of the office of teacher of boys, which has developed throughout the country in the last half century owes much to your leadership."

The Bishop closed, "Of Mrs. Peabody, who throughout your service has been the center of charm, happiness and affection to boys, graduates, teachers and trustees, we think with love which reaches a deep and abiding reverence."

It was a remarkable scene, the ninety-year-old Bishop, bidding farewell to the eighty-three-year-old Headmaster, both of them youthful in spirit, alert in mind, and strong in character.

The Bishop was through as President of the Board, but the Trustees could not let him leave without an expression of their feeling for him. Accordingly a cheque was given to him with the following letter, which tells the story of Bishop Lawrence's service to Groton.

It is difficult to think of you as subject to Time. Some of us are under the impression that you always existed. Certainly the mind of every Trustee of Groton School runneth not to the contrary. . . . Through two generations we have looked to you for wisdom spoken in season, for prudence without taint of time-serving, for understanding of the ways of boys—and men. "What will the Bishop say?" has become a reflex of our thought. . . .

This letter is between friends, and in it eulogy has no place. But at the conclusion of an association important in the lives of all of us, we wish to record our thankfulness that it has been given to us to know long and with intimacy a leader in whom Christian thought, Christian living and Christian charity are as the breath of his being. This has been an association which has encouraged the best in all of us, and perhaps, through its influence, even the worst of us has swerved a little toward the truth.

With feeling such as this, Bishop, we make you this modest

gift, knowing that in your hands it will be usefully employed; and the thought is in our minds that since the Chapel of the Massachusetts General Hospital is near your heart, you may wish to add in your own name to the fund provided for its maintenance this token payment of a debt which we can never hope to satisfy.

The Bishop was gratified at the choice of the Rev. John Crocker to succeed Dr. Peabody, but outside of personal relationships, he was through at Groton, true to his dictum, "When I am out, I am out."

Bishop Lawrence's interest in secondary education had for a primary motive his belief in the Christian religion as a spiritual force in the building of character. The Bishop was so many-sided that sometimes people did not always grasp that fact. He was often spoken of as an excellent business man, and he was. As a trustee, he was interested in many concerns – the maintenance of the buildings, the amount of the endowment, methods of investment, the scholarship of the boys. But it would be a grievous mistake to think for one moment that the Bishop had missed his calling. It was the spiritual welfare of the boys which held his first interest. What he wrote of Dr. Peabody was equally true of himself.

"The Rector does not wear his heart upon his sleeve, rather the opposite. He is a New Englander. He is unable in his modesty to enter into the details and technique of religion as some people can. His own life of comradeship with God, his reading and prayer in his study corner, and especially the school prayers and services in the very heart of the School, the Chapel, with the responses and singing of the boys, have all combined to give him strength and joy in his work."

The Bishop also had a remarkable connection with the Episcopal Theological School in Cambridge. His father had been an original Trustee of the School and was the donor of one of the dormitories, Lawrence Hall, where a tablet reads, in part, "For the use of godly youth studying here for the Ministry, this land was purchased and this hall was built by Amos Adams Lawrence, son of Amos, in 1872 and 1880 as a memorial of God's goodness to himself and to his family."

The Bishop was a member of the Class of 1875. In 1883 he returned to the School as Professor of Homiletics and of Pastoral Care, and in 1887 he became Dean. When he wrote a history of the School in 1940,[4] and sent it to Alumni and friends as a birthday gift on his ninetieth birthday, he referred in characteristic vein to his service as Professor.

The teaching of Homiletics and Pastoral Care was my school duty, besides alternating with the Dean in the Sunday morning sermon in the Chapel. I had also the pastoral care of some two hundred Harvard students, who had given their names to the Dean of the University as worshippers in St. John's Chapel. I also had a student Bible Class every Sunday in the College Yard, and the responsibility of a Sunday School of the children of the Chapel congregation, and undefined duties in assisting the Dean in the administration of the School.

Upon the death of Mr. Amory, I was given the duty of soliciting money to meet deficits. With great timidity I began work, for no trace of scholarship was ever found upon me. Until my Senior year at Harvard I had never really studied: at school and college I was always in the last half of the class. I matured late, and here I was, at thirty-three years of age a teacher of men only a few years younger than myself. Of

[4] *Seventy-three Years of the Episcopal Theological School, Cambridge* (1940), pp. 20–21.

Pastoral Care I could speak from experience, for during eight years I had worked with and practically lived with the working people of a large mill city. Of Homiletics I had had in preaching in my Lawrence parish for eight years the experience of a very limited success and frequent failure. The spiritual care of Harvard students brought happy friendships and often meagre results. And when in three years I was made Vice-Dean, and upon Dean Gray's retirement, at the end of four years I was made Dean, I wondered then, and have never ceased to wonder why. Sometimes I have thought that because I was not a scholar nor concentrated upon one subject, they assumed that I would have a free and unbiassed oversight of all subjects and their limitations.

The Bishop's estimate of his own capabilities, written over fifty years after the event, is over-modest, as many leaders of the Church will gladly testify. He was a helpful teacher, and his work as Dean was so successful that in 1893, upon the death of Phillips Brooks, he was elected Bishop of the Diocese of Massachusetts. As Bishop, he was Chairman of the Board of Visitors, and kept in close touch with the affairs of the School. In 1922–23 he with Dean Washburn led in raising the sum of $1,000,000 as an endowment.

This recital of facts cannot give the atmosphere of the Bishop's relationship to the School. Here was an association with his father, here he spent many of the happiest and most formative years of his life. Close at hand he had watched generation after generation of the students of the School, including his two sons, go out into positions of leadership and of responsibility in Church and in community. He wrote in sending out his history, "Having known more or less intimately the Founder of the School, every one of its Officers, Teachers and Graduates, being also its oldest living alumnus, I am on this May 30th, 1940, my ninetieth birthday, sending you this Sketch of the History of the School in which my father and I have taken deep interest from its beginnings. This story goes to you not only as a bit of local history, but also as a narrative of one of the many happy episodes of my favored life."

What countless memories of the Bishop come back to an alumnus of the School! In the morning of Commencement Day, it was his custom to receive the diplomas from the hand of the President of the Board, a layman, and to present them to the graduates. Then, to the very last of his life, he would give a short address, touching upon various aspects of the Ministry, but almost always stressing Truth and Liberty as illustrated by the experience of his own life.

Then would follow the luncheon on the lawn, where he had the opportunity to greet old students and friends who turned to him from all over the world for counsel and advice; for innumerable graduates never made a major move without consulting the Bishop. The truth is that so many talked to him that often he would go to Harvard Square for a more peaceful lunch in a restaurant by himself. Perhaps he would take a nap in the Deanery, returning for the Alumni meeting in the afternoon.

In the evening, the Bishop would speak at the dinner of the Alumni. It was usually an address of reminiscence. Honesty compels the admission that it was apt to be the same speech, but it was like a symphony which never grows old, which one can hear again and again. No one could tell of the past with greater charm or candor than the Bishop. Since he has passed from our sight, for many of us the dinner can never be just the same. He in a special way felt himself in a congenial family group.

He liked to tell anecdotes of the professors, and of the early life of the School. "Steenstra (Professor of Old Testament Exegesis) grew every month of his years of service. One afternoon, as we were passing from a Matriculation service to the dinner, I saw Professor Steenstra breaking away from the company and going home. I called to him to come back to dinner. He refused, saying, 'I must go and write my lecture for tomorrow.' 'Why don't you give your last year's lecture?' I asked. 'Because I don't believe it!' "[5]

One of his favorite stories had to do with the widow of Benjamin Tyler Reed, the founder. Mr. Reed had left a large legacy to the School, to be received at the death of Mrs. Reed, who had the income for her life. Mrs. Reed was some thirty or forty years younger than her husband. "Dean Stone made a call of condolence upon the widow. As he entered the drawing room, she greeted him warmly with the words, 'Oh, Doctor, don't you wish that I were dead, too?' At which the handsome old gentleman straightened himself, and exclaimed, 'O Queen, live forever!' whereupon she did." At the end of his address, the Bishop would receive an affectionate ovation from the Alumni, and would usually slip out for a quiet evening at home.

With all the Deans of the School who followed him, Bishop Lawrence was on terms of intimacy. Dean Hodges, in introducing him, used to compare himself to Bishop Lawrence by referring to the window in a Philadelphia church to the memory of Charles the Martyr. Outside in

[5] *Seventy-three Years*, pp. 14–15.

the Square stood a statue of William Penn. The window remarked, "William, they look up to you, but they see through me." Dean Washburn had been a student of the Bishop's in the School, and was one of his closest friends in the Diocese. One of the Bishop's last acts at the School was to institute the Reverend Angus Dun as Dean.

Bishop Lawrence had these close ties of affection and of association with the School in Cambridge, but his deeper interest was in the cause of theological education. In 1940 he wrote to the Church Divinity School of the Pacific,[6] which under great difficulties was struggling to make progress:

> I have written and spoken to California laymen, asking them how long they are going to build Cathedrals and Churches, and neglect to supply them with native spiritual leadership: a school for the great West can and will be built up; and it must be done not by the East or the whole Church, but by the West itself. The very work and sacrifice will make the best foundation. For years I gave my strength to the gathering of funds for the Episcopal Theological School in Cambridge. Hard, grinding, personal work by Dean, Bishops and laymen is demanded. Years, decades, generations may be consumed, but to my mind there is no greater or finer work to be done in this country than the upbuilding of an adequate school for the preparation of adequate spiritual leadership between the Rockies and the Pacific. God bless you and this work.

The response of the Church Divinity School to this letter reveals the high regard in which Bishop Lawrence was held: "It nerves us afresh to know that the 'First Citizen of the Episcopal Church,' three thousand miles away, feels so strongly the need of the Church Divinity School in the life of the Church as a whole."

[6] *Bulletin of the Church Divinity School of the Pacific*, June 1940.

But deepest of all came the Bishop's belief in the spiritual purposes of the Christian ministry. He saw the seminaries as means to a more important end. "I believe," he wrote, "that this country needs as never before men who are dedicated and intelligently consecrated to God and the service of their fellow men; who have such faith in a living God that they unconsciously connect religious faith with the every-day tests of life, and who are yet human enough to be in the closest and most sympathetic relations with all sorts of people. And I believe that this School [in Cambridge] is sending out such men, and should send out more. We need more of the heroic in life, and in many of our graduates we have it, often unheard of and unsung, in little country parishes, in great cities, in foreign lands." [7]

In his history of the Cambridge School, he gave his hope for the future:

> If old men do not dream dreams, young men will not see visions.
>
> May I set before you my dream of the School five, twenty-five, seventy-five years hence?
>
> 1. A School as it now is, but with steadily rising standards of thought and consecration, with ever increasing numbers of devoted teachers, and with graduates moving out into the parishes and missions.
>
> 2. There are infinite riches in our search for fresh revelations of a living God. Am I right in saying that while the literature of science and philosophy has increased greatly in this last half century, the scholarly literature of religion and of the interpretation of the Christian Faith has shrunk? This School should have scholars of such erudition, imagination and spiritual vision as will, while building up the faith of future leaders, send literature to interpret for the whole people faith in a living God, and the Glory of Him who is the Truth.

[7] *Seventy-three Years*, pp. 32–33.

3. Our Church is an organization; it is given practical things to do. As economic, social and religious conditions change, a Theological School should be a leader in helping the officers and people of the Church in meeting them.

4. Every graduate, whatever his office in the Church may be, will have a heart sympathetic with the people; his love will go out to them all, and especially to those who are burdened and heavy laden. He will be a good shepherd who knows his sheep. Whether his work is known or unknown, he will strive to bring to all faith, charity and peace.

A harassed world beckons us to supreme faith and devotion in the name of our Master, Jesus Christ.[8]

If Bishop Lawrence's relationship to Groton and the School at Cambridge was unusual, even more so was his connection with Harvard University. He was a graduate of Harvard College in the Class of 1871, and later served the University in one official capacity or another, for a total of forty-one years: Preacher, 1888–1891 and 1910–1913; Overseer, 1894–1906 and 1907–1912; Fellow, 1913–1931.

Most of this service occurred prior to his retirement as Bishop in 1927, and the story is told in his autobiography. Readers of *Memories of a Happy Life* will recall that in 1923 Dean Donham of the Harvard Graduate School of Business Administration asked Bishop Lawrence to be chairman of a committee to raise five million dollars for the School. This the Bishop, after some hesitation, undertook to do. The objectives of this committee were almost immediately expanded to include an effort to raise three million dollars for the Department of Chemistry and two million dollars for the Division of Fine Arts of the University. The "Committee to Extend the National Service of the Univer-

[8] *Seventy-three Years*, pp. 34–35.

sity" undertook to raise this amount. In the course of the campaign the Bishop approached Mr. George F. Baker of New York for a gift of one million dollars for the Business School. Before Mr. Baker gave his decision, the committee had secured about $1,250,000. Mr. Baker called on Bishop Lawrence at Mrs. Reed's house in New York.

"Bishop," he said, "I have been thinking over the matter of the Business School. I have lost interest in your suggestion that I should give the first million. I am not going to give it or half a million either. . . . If, however, by giving five million dollars I could have the privilege of building the whole School, I should like to do it. . . . I want to do it alone. Do you think that Harvard will let me?"[9]

This gift the University welcomed with joy as it did the success of the whole campaign and the resulting modernization of the laboratories of Chemistry and the building of the new Fogg Art Museum.

In the succeeding years Bishop Lawrence watched with deep interest the erection of these buildings and particularly of the Business School group across the Charles River near Soldiers Field. Finally, on June 4, 1927, the anticipated day of dedication arrived, another realization of Bishop Lawrence's dreams and hopes. The Bishop described the event in his diary:

> Saturday, June 4. Lovely day. 11.00 A.M. met at School, officers, Mr. Baker, etc. Band marched to platform in front of Library; probably 1,000 to 1,500 in chairs on lawn: wonderful transformation in three years. I offered Prayer of Dedication: Owen Young gave fine address: singing by Glee Club. Mr. Baker presented keys to President Lowell in a few beautiful

[9] *Memories of a Happy Life*, p. 420.

words with broken voice. President also beautifully received them, holding Mr. Baker with arm over his shoulders. Most simple and beautiful. Lunch in Faculty Club. Talk with many people. George Baker, Jr., said, "How do you like your baby?" I said, "It is not my baby. I was simply present at the birth." "Not a bit," he answered, "I want you to know that it was you who led my father to give the Foundation: your presentation of it to him, the needs, the opportunity, your way of doing it was what led him to make the gift. Don't you ever forget that." Mr. Baker, Sr., said later, "You know that this School would never have been except for you. You did it." Very gratifying.

2.30 P.M.: Company assembled again. Pres. presided. I gave first address, then Ex-Dean Gay: Dean Donham: Mr. Baker stayed through, and took 5 P.M. train for New York. A very successful and happy day, especially for Mr. Baker, and Donham and myself. Julia was there in the afternoon. Mr. Baker told her he had brought on a box of flowers for her, but our house shut, so he "had to give it to another girl."

The Bishop's address on this occasion was entitled "The George F. Baker Foundation: an Appreciation." [10] He told the story of how Mr. Baker desired to give the whole sum himself, saying, "This great gift of buildings came to the University not at the instigation of any committee or person, but upon the initiative of George F. Baker himself. He alone had the imagination to grasp the whole conception of this enterprise." The Bishop described the ideal which led Mr. Baker to make the gift. No doubt this was Mr. Baker's, but it is easy to imagine that the same ideal played an important part in Bishop Lawrence's appeal for a gift to the School.

"He sees thousands of young men coming from colleges throughout the country, meeting here to study and to

[10] *Harvard Business Review*, July 1927, pp. 395–396.

learn, as far as the conditions of this school can encompass it, the basic principles of business, its relation to society and to human welfare; to gain a fuller knowledge of economics, of the best methods of business in their various departments, and to be imbued with ideals and ambitions which will send them forth as teachers in other schools and in practical business life with a better sense of their responsibility to their calling and society, to earn a living, and perhaps make a fortune, always, however, sustaining the integrity and spirit of service which they have gained here. . . . The vision which was Mr. Baker's is now ours, that of a young nation entering upon higher standards of business and leading the world's civilization to richer life and greater happiness."

Five years later Bishop Lawrence was made very happy when a group of friends, including Dean Donham, presented his portrait by Mrs. Ellen Emmet Rand to the Graduate School of Business Administration.[11] There was a dinner party preceding the presentation. The chairman, Mr. Arthur W. Sewall of Philadelphia, stressed "the obligations of us all to Bishop Lawrence," and emphasized the action of "a clergyman who, understanding the real meaning of business in the proper sense, had done his best to advance its cause." Other speakers were Dean Donham and President Lowell. The Bulletin of the Harvard Business School Alumni Association summarized the Bishop's response:

Bishop Lawrence, when he thanked his friends for what was being done, talked in a way that made his hearers feel as though they had been copartners with him in the great work which he

[11] Another portrait of the Bishop hangs in the Harvard Union, near the portrait of his father.

did for the School. As to his share in the work of obtaining funds for the present foundation, he was far too modest. He implied that he had not had overmuch to do with it and showed a constant tendency to give the credit to others, but this was received by the audience with a respectful and cordial incredulity. . . .

On this most auspicious occasion a good man was honored and praised as he deserved, gratitude was expressed to him, recognition of great service was gladly given, but Bishop Lawrence himself would be the first to insist that past the friendship and appreciation the meeting showed, it evidenced the knowledge of all those present that a great change had come in economic and political life in the United States, a change of such proportions that every man, every agency, every institution in the country must do their utmost to make it not a change for the worse, but for the better. In this serious task it was plain that all understood that the School must play its part steadfastly and courageously.[12]

The Bishop's friendship with Dean Donham and his association with the Business School was always a source of gratification to him. He possessed a great deal of the business judgment and acumen of his forebears. In his various campaigns he enjoyed his New York office and his association with men of affairs. It is, indeed, unusual when a clergyman does as much for the world of business as did the Bishop.

For eighteen years Bishop Lawrence was a member of the Harvard Corporation, a self-perpetuating board of seven members. He summarized the duties of the Corporation in his autobiography.[13]

"The duties are those, not of an executive, but of coun-

[12] November 1932, p. 16.
[13] *Memories of a Happy Life*, pp. 416–417.

sellor to the President, who is the executive. The questions coming before the meetings relate to every subject connected with the University, from the purchase or sale of a piece of real estate to the appointment of a Professor of Philosophy. Every appointment to scholarship, fellowship, or teaching office, every item of the budget, passes through the Corporation. And to the Fellows the President gives in advance his plans for future development which may not come in practical working or before the public for years; or which may call for decision then and there."

Next to his family and the Church in the Bishop's heart and life came the University. It used to be said jokingly that he might speak critically of the House of Bishops, but not of the Harvard Corporation. When he was asked how seven men, all but one Bostonians, could retain control of an institution with the number of distinguished graduates possessed by Harvard, his answer would be, "It works. When a situation arises which needs quick action such as the gift of Mr. Harkness, we can act quickly."

Every concern of the University through the years touched him deeply. Several times after his retirement as Bishop he attempted to resign, but each time he was persuaded to continue. In 1931, however, he insisted. While he felt young and active, he realized that he was eighty-one years of age, and furthermore that President Lowell's term was drawing to a close, and that younger men should make the choice of the next President.

He wrote in his diary of his last meeting:

Monday, May 11, 1 P.M.: Harvard Overseers' Meeting at Lowell House: lunched with them: then to University Hall: Corporation — only four of us present. Pres. had my letter of resignation, which was accepted. Corporation voted to give me an Hon. LL.D. and Overseers confirmed it. A very great honor, too great; and gratified as I was, I protested that it should not be; but they insisted. I have already an S.T.D. from Harvard in 1893. Only Mark Hopkins, Lord Bryce and Pres. Eliot have been thus honored, so far as is known. I don't understand why I should have such honors and degrees which belong to scholars and great leaders. But I fell to the temptation, and gratefully yielded.

7.30. Back at the President's house for Annual Overseers' dinner. Home quite depressed at thought of end of all official relations with Harvard, longer than anyone in a century except Charles W. Eliot. Am content that I am wise to retire when I am well and strong, and except for my years I believe all want me to remain. I must now set my mind to be happy in quiet, friendly family relations, helping a bit here and there. Must forget myself in others.

In the following month Bishop Lawrence received the honorary degree of Doctor of Laws, with the citation from President Lowell, "William Lawrence: Bishop of Massachusetts for thirty-three years, and for eighteen a member of the Corporation. Wise, large, and tolerant in the many duties that have come in a singularly useful and happy life."

The Bishop's degree was presented last. When he stood, the whole audience rose and applauded, testifying to the affection in which he was held by the Harvard family.

Bishop Lawrence in his address [14] described in detail and in high praise the administration of President Lowell. He began with a reference to President Eliot, and the expansion of the elective system. He then quoted from President Lowell's inauguration address: "Our American Universities do not strive enough in the impressionable years of early

[14] *Harvard Alumni Bulletin*, June 1931.

manhood to stimulate intellectual appetites and ambitions, nor do they foster productive scholarship enough among members of their staffs who are capable thereof. Education is not knowledge: it is an attitude of mind." The Bishop said, "As we walked away together, I said, 'Lawrence, that is a pretty sharp break with the past.' 'Not at all,' was his reply. 'It is the same old ship, only on another tack.' He has been the captain of the old ship: the reach of that task has been twenty-two years; and now I ask you to join with me for a few minutes as we take our bearings."

Continuing, the Bishop told of Dr. Lowell's development of the academic and spiritual life of the University; the concentration of the students' interest upon one field of work, and a general final examination on that field as a test of education; the growth of the tutorial system, and the consequent increase in the quality of scholarship; the wise selection of teachers; the strengthening of the University finances, and especially of the Graduate Schools; the erection of new buildings, especially the Houses made possible by the gift of Mr. Edward S. Harkness; and finally the founding of the Society of Fellows.

The Bishop concluded, "Brethren of the Alumni, next autumn the new Chapel will rise to stand as a symbol of that upon which Harvard was founded – faith in the Living God as revealed in His Son Jesus Christ. Her highest purpose is to mold character, to create men of faith, truth, courage and serenity. In the strain and pressure of today, I believe, and I say with all the conviction in my power, that a young man whose life is immersed in the Living God, who has given himself completely to the service of Jesus Christ, and is ready to stand with Him Who said, 'Ye seek to kill me, a man that hath told you the truth,' has a force and a charm which no other life can give.

"President Lowell: for twenty-two years your hand has been steady and strong on the helm of the old ship. Whether the reach of this tack be short or long, we sons of Harvard hail you and bid you Godspeed – Our Captain."

Thus ended Bishop Lawrence's official connection with the University, but as long as he lived he continued to be regarded by Harvard men with affection as a wise elder statesman. On Armistice Day, 1932, the Harvard Memorial Church was dedicated, and it was natural that Bishop Lawrence should be selected as the preacher for that service.[15]

He recalled the long history of the University from John Harvard to the youngest alumnus. "We note one line of cleavage that is between the men who in time lived only for their day, pleasure or profit, and those who with longer sight and higher vision lived for the future, for others, for ideals."

In the World War three hundred and seventy-three of the sons of Harvard gave their lives. The Bishop continued, "In the dedication of this Chapel and of the Porch, on whose walls the names of the dead are written in gold, we set these forth in our minds, the chosen of them all, who had the glory of making the supreme sacrifice."

The Bishop discussed the motives of these men, pointing out "that each one had his own vision, his own path of duty, his own faith and line of action." He quoted from a letter of a Harvard boy to his mother. "Mother, dear, I

[15] *Harvard Alumni Bulletin*, November 18, 1932.

feel no bitterness against the Huns as individuals or as a race. It is war that I hate, and war that I am willing to give all to end as permanently as possible, for it isn't the men that war kills: it is the mother's heart which it destroys that makes it hateful to me."

"Because the sons of Harvard have faith, want more faith, and believe in the constant nurture of faith, they have given this Chapel to the University. They have so planned that as the students enter the Chapel, they will pass through a porch saturated with the atmosphere of faith, faith in the truth, in liberty, in love, in justice and a readiness to sacrifice their best in the search for and attainment of the objects of that faith."

The Bishop urged that the Chapel stand through the years as a power for the increase of faith in the unseen, and for the establishment of peace.

Bishop Lawrence was at his best in informal addresses of a biographical nature. He had the gift of an excellent memory, the ability to stress the unusual detail, and a certain candor, all of which made his subject live. One of the best examples of Bishop Lawrence as a delineator of character is given by his address on Charles William Eliot before the Harvard Teachers Association in 1934.[16]

He began by telling of his first memory of President Eliot, when he saw him row No. 3 in the Harvard Crew of 1858, adding this note, "The handkerchiefs tied around the heads of the crew, which had been bought by Charles Eliot just before the race, set forever the Harvard color, crimson."

[16] *Harvard Teachers Record*, April 1934.

He described Mr. Eliot's loneliness as a student and his austerity as a young President. "With a straight backbone, and as some felt, a stiff neck, he walked through the Yard from Chapel to University Hall, to his house, looking neither to the right nor left, but always conscious of what was before and about him. Short-sighted, he did not easily recognize professors or students, and the common feeling was that he had no human interest in them. Not so. As I was walking with him once from Chapel to University Hall, we passed a student whom I knew and bowed to, the President looking straight ahead. He then turned to me and said, 'What do you know about that young man?' speaking his name. He knew him, but from habit or bashfulness or reserve had given no evidence of it." The Bishop stated that this impression of austerity was false, that "the cramped house of the President was the college infirmary."

Bishop Lawrence spoke of Dr. Eliot's courage in battling for his ideals. "One remark of Eliot's at his ninetieth anniversary is illuminating. President Lowell in a three-minute address laid stress upon only one characteristic, his moral courage; to which Eliot responded (I quote from memory) 'I had no idea that I have had especial moral courage. I only know that when I have before me an object which must be attained, and I know that its attainment is right, I move steadily towards that object. . . . If that is moral courage, so be it.' " This statement was often quoted by Bishop Lawrence as evidence of Dr. Eliot's character and determined leadership.

The Harvard Tercentenary Celebration in 1936 gave Bishop Lawrence great delight. It is safe to say that not even the youngest alumnus enjoyed all the proceedings as much as he did. He took it all in, almost from beginning to the end, having as his house guests Dr. Charles Harold Dodd, the great New Testament scholar of Cambridge University, England, and Dr. Charles R. Brown, the Dean Emeritus of the Yale Divinity School. He attended the reception by President Conant to the great number of distinguished guests, officiated with others at the Service of Thanksgiving in the Harvard Memorial Church, went to the meeting of the Harvard Alumni Association, and the Symphony concert at Sanders Theatre in memory of Henry Lee Higginson; was present at a dinner at Eliot House given by Professor Roger Merriman, and the fireworks afterward on the Charles River. All this was undertaken by the Bishop sixty-five years after his own graduation from the University.

Bishop Lawrence described the events of the final day in his diary:

Friday, September 18. A.M.: Cloudy, and by 10.30 began to rain, and through exercises rained steadily, though not heavily; but as last hymn was sung and my benediction, it came heavily and with wind, so no recessional, and the afternoon session in open theatre was abandoned; held in Sanders Theatre.

9.30 A.M.: As Marshal, with my '71 standard in front of University: having cut the back of my hand on a door, went to "Red Cross," got it fixed up by a nurse. Went back and marched with standard in hand; also baton and overcoat on my arm: beaver hat: no classmates to keep me company. 1860–62 had banner for absent members: others had young men carry the standard, then one or two for each class; then followed the successive standards of hundreds of alumni. The Honorary degrees, distinguished delegates, came from Widener Hall, some 400 or 500 in gowns; brilliant color; wonderful order and promptness. At my class seat, left my standard with an aide: went to Preachers' room: left hat: put on Harvard gown and hood, and Oxford cap: went out and around to Widener Hall, joined procession again, and went up onto the platform, which held the several hundred guests, delegates, etc. Then President Roosevelt, supported by aides, came in from Chapel and took seat in front row. President Conant in President's chair in centre, President Roosevelt on his right, I on Roosevelt's right, Lawrence Lowell on my right. As it had begun to rain, aides gave us umbrellas. I offered mine to Roosevelt, who said that he wanted to encourage the silk hat trade, and to feel as if he were fishing; and he sat without cover in the falling rain from 10 until 1: Lawrence would not let me put down my umbrella, so except for our knees, were covered. A moment of silence, and then the bells of St. Saviour's Church, Southwark, pealed out as gloriously and clear as if we were on London Bridge: almost a miracle. Then followed the addresses and chorus. Conant made a very fine oration: then 62 distinguished scholars from all over the world received the Hon. Doctor's degree. Perfect in order and dignity: each degree with citation took only thirty seconds. Then followed, "O God our help, etc." I stepped up upon the rostrum and gave the Benediction. Jerome Greene asked if I would lunch quickly in the Preachers' Room with President R. After Gov. Curley came out, I went in. We had a pleasant, informal talk about the Appletons of the Chapel, Groton School, President Eliot, etc., and at 2.25 we started for Sanders Theatre in the driving rain. Was taken to a chair in front of stage. Lawrence Lowell presided: excellent addresses of high order. At 5 the meeting adjourned, and I paddled across the Yard in the beaver hat and dress suit, to Weld 29, where I found a bottle of hot soup. Then home in motor. Apart from the storm, it was a very great occasion and ceremony, the detail so perfect that it even conquered the storm.

In the midst of the rain, a friend met the Bishop and tried to persuade him to enter her car, lest he catch cold. He refused, saying, "The Lord will not let me catch cold on Harvard's three-hundredth birthday."

AT THE HARVARD TERCENTENARY
1936

Bishop Lawrence's last appearance at a Harvard Commencement was in June, 1941, when Lord Halifax, the British Ambassador, held a Convocation of Oxford University and gave an honorary degree to President Roosevelt, who was represented by an aide. "It was," the Bishop wrote, "a red-letter day for me," for he was given the Harvard Alumni Medal "for great service to the University," and it happened that the President of the Alumni Association, who awarded the medal, was his great-nephew, Leverett Saltonstall, Governor of Massachusetts.

"This medal," he said, "will be presented today to a distinguished Member of the Class of 1871, who is attending this year his eightieth Harvard Commencement either as a guest, an undergraduate, a graduate, or an office-holder of the University. In that period of time he has served Harvard notably and conscientiously in many different capacities and in addition, has been a distinguished leader of the Episcopal Church, and a worthy citizen of this Commonwealth and of the United States." [17]

With this high point, Bishop Lawrence's long connection with Harvard came to an end. How Harvard men felt toward him is expressed in a letter from Mr. Langdon P. Marvin, President of the Harvard Club of New York.

> Every Harvard man owes you a debt of gratitude for all that you have been to and done for the University and its Alumni during these many years, and for your friendship and help. You have the high respect and the deep affection of the whole Harvard Family as few others have ever had them. Your position in the Harvard Family is unique.

[17] *Harvard Alumni Bulletin*, July 5, 1941.

VI

The Church Beyond The Diocese

FOR YEARS, ever since his consecration in 1893, Bishop Lawrence had played a leading role in the affairs of the Protestant Episcopal Church. When he resigned as Bishop of Massachusetts in 1927, while his interest never abated, his activity became less as the years passed. For some time he retained his membership in the National Council, the body which has financial responsibility between triennial sessions of the General Convention, the final authority on all Church affairs; and he still continued as president of the Church Pension Fund. His last important mission for the Church was in 1928, after Mrs. Lawrence's death, when he became Bishop in charge of the European Churches.

The Protestant Episcopal Church has a number of parishes in various European cities. There is no resident Bishop, and these churches are under the supervision of the Presiding Bishop, who arranges for visitations from time to time. Bishop Murray, then the Presiding Bishop, asked Bishop Lawrence to act for him. It cannot be said that at this time the trip was of great ecclesiastical significance; but it was important that some Bishop should go, and Bishop Lawrence was a distinguished representative of the

American Episcopate. For him it meant a change, particularly the opportunity of seeing old friends abroad. He was happy that his daughter, Mrs. Morton Fearey, could go with him, as well as his son and daughter-in-law, the Rev. and Mrs. Frederic Lawrence, who had just been married in Washington. For them it was a honeymoon trip.

The party sailed from New York in early April and went directly to Paris, where the Bishop at once took up Church affairs with Dean Beekman of the Cathedral of the Holy Trinity. The Bishop was particularly interested in the new student center, in his visit to the Latin Quarter, and in the work of St. Luke's Chapel, carried on by the Rev. and Mrs. H. R. Wadleigh. He formed a less favorable opinion of the quality of many of the so-called students, for his comment in his diary was: "Impressed by dangers, moral conditions, for young American men and women – an atmosphere of affected Bohemianism, and a question whether many of them really have talent, but are the restless and rather lighter quality of American students." The Bishop especially enjoyed a dinner with the former Ambassador to the United States, M. Jules Jusserand, and Madame Jusserand, who was related to the Bishop. M. Jusserand was the intimate friend of President Theodore Roosevelt, as was Bishop Lawrence. The Bishop reported that the former Ambassador "was scintillating with bright talk, showed us Washington document given him by President Coolidge, also certificate of election to tennis cabinet of Roosevelt, signed, both framed in his drawing room."

After a few days spent arranging for the coming Convocation, the Lawrence party left for Nice, where the Bishop administered the rite of Confirmation; then, by way of Genoa, they went to Rome and to Florence, stopping at Perugia en route. There were the usual services, conferences, receptions, and sight-seeing, after which they traveled to Geneva by way of Milan.

The Bishop all his life enjoyed associations with the past, and was delighted to find himself in the hotel where he had stayed with his father and family just sixty-one years before. The Bishop had not been an advocate of the League of Nations, but while in Geneva he visited the League of Nations Building, where the Committee on Economics was meeting, with Mr. Roland Boyden of Massachusetts in attendance.

Then followed two weeks in Paris, taken up by various activities of work and of play. The Bishop visited the Russian Church Theological Seminary, in which his sister, Mrs. Cunningham, had been so greatly interested. This was the only Seminary left to the Russian Church after the Revolution. A brave and consecrated group of students lived there, amid great poverty and hardship, studying under a remarkable faculty of which one of the best known was Father Sergius Boulgakoff. The Bishop wrote in his diary,

To Russian Church Theol. Academy. Welcomed by the Metropolitan, and address by Rev. Father Boulgakoff, who read an address of welcome, mentioning Hetty C.'s name. Interpreter translated it for others. Singing by the choir, very impressive. Then the Chapel: two altars. Lutheran Chapel now entirely Russian, icons, etc. Living rooms, 10 or 12 beds in a room: very bare: also refectory. Evidently very poor but intelligent, cheerful and courteous. Stayed over an hour. Picturesque sight, about 40 students.

The next day the Convocation opened, with Bishop Lawrence as the presiding officer. The Bishop commented very practically, "Good discussion, excellent spirit, much variety of opinion as to practical propositions. Much talk what the field needed and kind of man: not much on ways and means."

On May 30th, Bishop Lawrence celebrated his seventy-eighth birthday. There was a Memorial Day service in the Cathedral, attended by Ambassador Herrick, British Ambassador Crewe, a representative of the French President, and organizations of all sorts. Bishop Lawrence in his address spoke of the spirit of America and of France, as exemplified in Abraham Lincoln and Lafayette. "Sons of America, brethren of all the Allied Nations, as on this Memorial Day we lay our wreaths upon the graves, let us each and all treasure this truth in days of peace. The glory of life is not to get but to give, not to rule but to serve, not to save our life but to lose it in winning for others the finer life." In the afternoon, Bishop Lawrence went to Suresnes Cemetery for another memorial service. There were sixteen hundred graves of American soldiers there. Ambassador Herrick and others made addresses, and seventy-five French orphan girls sang.

The following day, the Bishop and his family arrived in London, and soon the Bishop went to call on his old friend Dr. Leighton Parks, for many years the Rector of Emmanuel Church, Boston, later of St. Bartholomew's Church, New York, and now retired, making his permanent home in England.

Perhaps the highlight of the whole trip was the Bishop's visit to Archbishop and Mrs. Davidson, first at Canterbury, and then at Lambeth Palace. Bishop and Mrs. Lawrence had visited the Davidsons in Winchester in 1897, when the Archbishop was Bishop of Winchester. In 1904, the Archbishop and Mrs. Davidson came to the United States to attend the General Convention in Boston, and visited the Lawrences in Bar Harbor and in Boston. In turn, the Lawrences were guests of the Davidsons during the succeeding Lambeth Conferences for all the Bishops of the Anglican Communion. Thus, with more or less frequent correspondence, had been cemented a close friendship of thirty years' standing. Bishop Lawrence was deeply moved at being once again with these greatly admired old friends, especially because of memories of previous visits when Mrs. Lawrence had been with him. He wrote for the *Boston Transcript* [1] an estimate of the Archbishop which revealed his admiration.

> Randall Davidson has in him the temper of a statesman. When the issues of right and wrong are clear, he never hesitates. He has moral courage: if necessary, he will stand alone. But throughout his life he has been a leader who has felt it of the highest importance to carry his army along with him. He has, therefore, while holding his ideals, kept in close touch with the temper of the English people and of the Church; and as the highest officer of the Church, has felt bound to bring the Church to move with him. There have been occasions when those who looked on and did not know all the conditions have felt that he gave too much consideration to the opinions of the Conservatives, whether in national education, social and political problems, or Church administration. But the event has usually justified his wisdom.

At the time of Bishop Lawrence's visit, the matter of the Revision of the Book of Common Prayer of the Church of England was before Parliament, and feeling ran high. In

[1] Saturday, Aug. 4, 1928.

England, because the Church of England is established, Parliament has the final authority, even in matters of deeply spiritual concern, and Parliament was made up of members of every religious faith or of no faith at all. The Church had agreed upon the form the proposed Book should take; the House of Lords had acted favorably, and the question was soon to come before the House of Commons. Many felt at the time that the spiritual liberty of the Church was at stake.

But to return to the Bishop's visit to the Archbishop.

Monday, June 4. Took train for Canterbury. Archbishop's motor met us and took us to the "Old Palace." Warm reception by Miss Mills and by Mrs. Davidson, who kissed me and Julie. Archbishop in bed: has been ill a week. After lunch to see Archbishop in bed, who held out his two hands, saying, "I have been wanting to see you and have looked forward to this. How well and young you look!" He had his candidates and ordination last week, and Sunday. Has his Diocesan Synod in a few days, and on the 13th comes the great debate in Parliament on the adoption of the Prayer Book. "I never was so pressed with duties of the utmost importance requiring my best strength, and I have neither." After a short talk, I went with the others and Miss Mills, who showed us over the Cathedral. Most interesting and beautiful, of course. She knew what to call special attention to. Evensong going on, with the same minor chord of choir that we heard from the monks of Assisi. Back to Old Palace. Archbishop came to tea, and I had talk with him. Archbishop is older, of course ill now. Still he is full of wisdom and interested in all subjects; of course the Prayer Book debate is hanging over him, and he is entirely in the dark as to how the vote will go. He went to bed after tea. Dinner, talk and prayer in Chapel. Weather, damp, cold: also house.

In their conversation, the Archbishop and the Bishop discussed many matters, including the work of the Russian

Seminary in Paris, the opportunity of the American Episcopal Churches on the Continent, and closer coöperation between the Church of England and the Protestant Episcopal Church.

The method of administering the American European Churches had long been a matter of discussion. Bishop Brent, with his broad vision of the world, had felt that a distinguished American Bishop should be sent to Europe with permanent status as an ecclesiastical statesman in the finest sense. Bishop Lawrence, with his more practical sense, had doubted the wisdom of such an appointment. In this matter the Archbishop apparently agreed with Bishop Lawrence, for in a later letter to Bishop Brent he wrote,

> We saw Bishop Lawrence when he was in England a couple of months ago, and I thought him singularly young and vigorous. I am inclined to think that he and I agree more closely than you and I do about the intervention of American Episcopal action in the Continent of Europe and in the Near East. I am rather apprehensive of an American Bishop at work in those regions without having really enough to do, and consequently feeling himself called upon to exercise rather an embarrassing interference with such Anglican Episcopal action as exists.

Bishop Brent, however, was not wholly convinced, for upon Bishop Lawrence's return, he wrote to him,

> I have just finished reading your report. I think you are too cautious, but inasmuch as it is the policy of our Church to be cautious, perhaps I shouldn't and will not grouch. I recognize the difficulties of securing a competent man to fill a position when dual duties of widely diverse character would be necessary. At the same time, there is one fact that you do not recognize. The American Protestant Churches in Europe are pushing ahead. We alone are stagnant. I am still young enough in spirit to desire to see the Church make reasonable ventures.

To go back to Bishop Lawrence at Canterbury:

June 5. 8.45 A.M. Prayer. Breakfast. Mrs. Davidson asked me up to her room in top of house, talked of Julia; how she and Archbishop had been saying that the atmosphere of her presence always about, her umbrella, his sweater, her bed-watch, all from her. She wonderful in her poise and grace and simplicity, and more affectionate than ever.

Returning to London, the Lawrences and Mrs. Fearey went to Oxford for several days, where the Bishop was confined to his room because of stiffness in his back. In London again, Mrs. Fearey and the Bishop had luncheon at Lambeth Palace.

Archbishop and Mrs. Davidson in garden in sun: he looked pretty feeble: he solicitous for me. Walked a few minutes, then to lunch. Julie on his right, I on his left and next Mrs. Davidson: Archbishop of York on her left, two Chaplains, Miss Tait and Miss Mills. A very nice quiet chat, he entirely himself, of course anxious about debate in House today and tomorrow. No idea as to the result. Confident that if accepted Prayer Book will be loyally obeyed. Think he enjoyed our coming and forgot himself. She as bright and lovely as ever. I told her that her portrait by Lazlo did her injustice: made her look old and commonplace, which she never is: her face has an expression of alertness and charm which is unique — at which the Archbishop of York applauded, and said, "Hear, hear!" At my request, Miss Mills got the housekeeper whom Julia liked, and the old deaf manservant who has been there over fifty years, and I shook hands with them. Archbishop insisted on seeing us off. F. and K. came in taxi, and they all stood at door. Mrs. Davidson kissed me goodby: an affectionate parting from all, and they waved until we went out the gate. Very dear, simple and affectionate people, and at crisis of the Church and State, where he is in the centre, with affection and respect of Great Britain. Next his Sargent portrait is a framed original sketch from *Punch*, sent from the whole staff, depicting Archbishop standing on Prayer Book as a raft, in full robes, in utmost serenity.

As is well known, the proposed Prayer Book was defeated in the House of Commons. Soon afterward the Archbishop resigned, being succeeded by the Archbishop of York, and was created Lord Davidson by the King. He and Bishop Lawrence never met again. But Bishop Lawrence, with Bishop Murray, the Presiding Bishop, and Bishop Brent, was instrumental in raising a sum of money which was presented to Archbishop and Mrs. Davidson upon his retirement, from friends in America.

On June 14, the Bishop and Mrs. Fearey sailed from Southampton. He still had great energy, despite his painful back, for he recorded:

June 15. The Revised Prayer Book rejected by House of Commons, 266–220. Sent cable of sympathy to Archbishop. Amused myself by writing a paper on "The Crisis of Church and State in England." May use it.

This article was the substance of a long interview with the Bishop upon his arrival in New York by a representative of the *New York Times*, but none of the forebodings of the time as to the future relationship of Church and State in England have as yet materialized.

On Tuesday, June 19, the ship docked at four in the afternoon; the Bishop took the midnight train for Boston, and was immediately at the familiar tasks. Few younger men, after a transatlantic trip, with the tedium of customs inspection and the midnight train, could record:

Slept all night. 6.50 A.M. Marian and Polly with Smith at station. To Sallie's for Breakfast: then to Cambridge, Corporation meeting at 9.45 until one.

Thus ended what the Bishop described as a "happy and successful trip."

Although Bishop Lawrence resigned as President of the Church Pension Fund in 1931, the progress of that remarkable institution was a source of joy and pride to him to the end of his life; for it was to him more than to any other single person that the Fund owed its existence.

His successor as President, Mr. William Fellowes Morgan, in his address at the Symphony Hall meeting in recognition of Bishop Lawrence's fortieth anniversary as Bishop, described the origin of the Fund with the appointment of a commission to consider the matter at the General Convention of 1910 in Cincinnati. Bishop Lawrence was made chairman of this commission, which established the program which was approved by the Convention of 1916, with the proviso that an initial reserve fund of five million dollars be raised before the Fund could actually begin operations.

To quote Mr. Morgan,

> Thus the General Convention gave Bishop Lawrence its blessing, and set him out to sea with instructions to raise five million dollars before he could function at all. He bravely undertook to raise a sum of money larger than had ever been attempted before in the Church. The Diocese of Massachusetts relieved him temporarily of his diocesan duties, and for over a year he spent his time untiringly in travelling about the Church from the little office that he established in Wall Street, and wherever he went, I remember, he always wore the same derby hat which he refused to put aside until the campaign for the initial reserve had been successfully concluded. It turned into an extremely valuable hat, being worth almost nine million dollars.[2]

The interesting story of the raising of this great sum and the establishment of the working principles of the Fund

[2] *A Harvest of Happy Years* (Boston and New York: Houghton Mifflin Co., 1933), pp. 7–8.

are not a part of the record of these later years of Bishop Lawrence, for the Fund commenced operations on March 1, 1917, and by 1927 had proved itself one of the most effective pension systems not only in the Church, but in the educational and business world as well. Bishop Lawrence followed its development every step of the way; for almost until his death he remained a Trustee, and was always an adviser to his successor as President, and to Monell Sayre and Bradford Locke, the executives of the Fund.

To show the magnitude of the Fund of which the Bishop was the founder, it is interesting to quote from the annual report of the President, Bishop Cameron Davis, in 1941, the year of Bishop Lawrence's death:

> On March 1, 1942, the Church Pension Fund will have completed a quarter century of active service. Beginning with an initial reserve of $8,800,000 secured from the Church by the leadership and personal effort of Bishop Lawrence, the assets at the end of 1941 were $35,650,000. This figure is "book value," reckoned on the basis required by the Insurance Department of New York State. The market value, however, of the invested assets would increase that figure substantially. Considering the facts that since its inception the Fund has paid out a total of approximately $21,000,000 in pension benefits, and that during this quarter of a century the world has known two wars and two economic depressions, the latest of which was the most severe in history, these figures are remarkable. The present Pension Roll includes the names of about 2,500 beneficiaries, and is at the rate of over $1,390,000 a year.

In addition, Bishop Davis reported that the Church Life Insurance Corporation had a net worth of $943,000, with $27,300,000 of insurance in force, insuring 8,250 individuals. The Church Properties Fire Insurance Corporation had a net worth of $439,000, with $97,000,000 worth of insurance in force. The Church Hymnal Corporation, formed wholly to be of service to the Church, had a net worth of $48,000. These three corporations are subsidiaries of the Church Pension Fund, and explain themselves by their titles. They were established through the years as the need became apparent. It is no wonder that Bishop Lawrence felt a justified pride in the accomplishment of the Fund.

But again it must be pointed out that the Bishop was not primarily interested in the Fund because great sums of money were involved. He cared for the spiritual purpose which was the motive power behind all of his effort and success. He thought of the efficiency of the clergy of the Church first. The financial appeal and later financial stability were in his eyes simply means to a much greater end – the spread of Christ's Kingdom throughout the world.

The Bishop made this clear in *Memories of a Happy Life.*[3]

Moved by sympathy at the suffering and poverty of the aged servants of the Church, bishops, clergy, laymen and women bemoaned conditions, declaimed at the injustice and made their appeals more and more pathetic. No body of persons dependent upon charity can long retain their self-respect. Men and women working in the fulness of their strength find ambition and efficiency weakened at the anticipation of falling into the charity class in their old age. As a member of the Board of Missions, I became more and more uneasy at the steadily mounting total of pensions voted for the retired missionaries or their families: a burden placed upon the future Church for work already done. But how could one protest at or criticise the gifts to these pathetic people or the system until he had something better to offer?

[3] Page 349.

The Bishop did have something better to offer, and as a result countless clergy and their wives will be grateful to him, and the Church will be more efficient. Here is a clergyman after the end of a lifetime of service facing old age with a weakening of his powers. Before the Pension Fund was established he had only two choices, either to continue until he dropped, with the parish going to pieces in the meantime, or else to be dependent upon charity. With the Pension Fund in operation, his various parishes have paid the pension premiums, and he is entitled to a pension. What this means to individuals and to the Church is almost incalculable, for in addition to retired clergy there are grants to widows and to orphan children.

At Bishop Lawrence's anniversary, Mr. Morgan presented him with a book of letters expressing the gratitude of beneficiaries. One old clergyman's letter is typical of many:

> I passed my seventy-third milestone on life's highway on the eighth of March, and while eager and willing to work, I have begun to feel the burden of doing that which has always been a joy to me. In the order of nature, and according to insurance statistics, I have an age expectancy of about seven years, so that I have little hope of being a charge upon the Pension Fund resources for many more years. It was indeed a most gracious act of the Pension Fund Trustees to give such consideration to the old way-worn veterans of the Church army, and I for one wish I could find words to express my most grateful appreciation of what they have done to make the last few miles of our journey easier for our tired feet. My heartiest thanks to you and all who have made life happier for me.

It should be added that in 1927 the Bishop himself became a beneficiary, for he did not wish to have the Fund regarded as a charity. Mr. Monell Sayre, the Executive Vice-President, wrote to him:

> You will give me permission to add to the formal statement that this pension is the most distinguished one it is possible for the Fund to grant, and that I and other members of the Executive Committee felt how delightful a thing it was for the Fund, and how dignifying to its operations that the roll of its beneficiaries should contain your name.

There is no doubt that through the years, in increasing service to the Church and to men, women, boys, and girls, the Church Pension Fund founded by Bishop Lawrence will stand as his greatest visible gift to the Church.

Bishop Lawrence was not content to rest, however, with the securing of pensions for the clergy alone. There are a great number of unordained Church workers serving throughout the world — doctors, teachers, nurses, deaconesses. These could not be included in the purpose of the original Fund, but the Bishop had them on his mind and heart in a way not generally known even today, since for various reasons, and especially because of the depression, his proposal to benefit them could not be carried through.

Bishop Lawrence had written to the Presiding Bishop in 1929 offering to give personally $50,000 if a sound actuarial scheme could be devised for pensions for these unordained workers, and sufficient money to take care of the accrued liabilities could be secured. Later on, he did contribute twenty-eight shares of Pacific Gas and Electric Company common stock, and sixty shares of General Electric Company common stock, stating in a letter to Dr. Lewis Franklin, Treasurer of the National Council, "These shares and the accumulated dividends will go towards my subscription of $50,000 in case the pension system for unordained missionaries should go through. But if it fails, then I am under no obligation for the $50,000; but of course whatsoever I shall have paid in will go to the credit of the National Council for such charitable aid of unordained missionaries as the Council decides."

The Bishop had been ready, though eighty years of age, to try to raise the accrued liabilities. He wrote characteristically, "It was understood that I undertake this unofficially and quietly, so that if the plan failed, it would not affect the Church or public confidence."

The proposal, however, was never undertaken, owing to unforeseen circumstances, and the Bishop was forced to withdraw the offer. "I write this of course with much regret, and hope that so long as the unordained missionaries are not protected by pension or life insurance, they will be a challenge to the Church's sense of justice and chivalry."

The Bishop gradually terminated all his official connections, including his membership on the National Council, but in 1932 he was again called into special service. The Church was facing a difficult financial crisis. At the General Convention of 1931, a budget of over four million dollars had been adopted. It was soon apparent that this figure was not to be met by the giving of the Church in a time of depression. The National Council was faced with two tasks: first, to rouse the constituency of the Church to make every effort to raise as much money as possible; and second, to begin a long and heart-breaking retreat in the reduction of the budget by hundreds of thousands of dollars. Unless one has been through such an experience, it is not easy to realize the difficulty of these tasks. On the one hand, people were irritated at such a time by constant appeals for gifts, while on the other, those in the missionary field were greatly depressed by the reduction in appropriations, especially as the budget was largely made up of the already low salaries of missionaries and workers all over the world.

When the House of Bishops met in Garden City in 1932, feeling on both sides ran high, and it was finally decided to appoint a special committee of the House of Bishops to confer with and to advise the National Council. Bishop Perry, the Presiding Bishop, appointed Bishop Davis of Western New York and Bishop McDowell of Alabama, and for the Chairmanship he turned naturally to Bishop Lawrence, who had the confidence of all because he had shown for many years both his interest in the missionary cause and his unfailing business judgment.

The details of the report of this committee are not of general interest at this late date. Suffice it to say that their work was of great value and assistance. For the purpose of this account, of greater interest are the general principles in a memorandum prepared by Bishop Lawrence for the use of the committee. The majority of his impressions are as true today as ten years ago.

He wrote:

The Church, and especially the National Council, is faced by a psychological situation, to meet which calls for as much thought as does the street financial condition. Due to various reasons, some of them founded on incorrect information, over-emphasis of certain points by the Church press and others, the national tendency to criticise those whose duty it is to plan the getting of money from others as well as spending it, the pressure of the cause by those who are intelligent as to the financial needs upon those who are ignorant and yet are depended upon to give, the inability of some of those who receive contributions to sense correctly the feelings of those who are expected to give, the natural comparison between different dioceses, with other reasons too many to mention, have been gradually leading the Church to feel that the pressure for money has been too high, that larger expenses have been entered into by their officers than the people were ready for, that adjustment towards economies have not been promptly carried through, and that the beginnings of a bureaucracy are now in sight.

This frame of mind we must meet. At the same time, the need of preaching the Gospel of Christ, the upbuilding of Christian character abroad and at home is enhanced by these very conditions; and those who have upon them the duty of carrying these things forward are keener than ever for such spiritual reinforcements as will increase the strength of the cause of Christ.

The immediate job of the Church is to democratize its giving constituency; and that must be done by building up as never before diocesan pride, self-respect, intelligence and devotion.

The Church has unfortunately gotten into the habit of thinking that if $1,000 is asked, we do well if we give $950: hence the total 100% is discounted in advance. I have the feeling that if we can put the figure so low that we are confident of going over the top, we can improve the morale of the Church. Some ardent and fine souls may think this figure shows lack of faith, a yielding to a selfish spirit: others will esteem it an honest recognition of a condition. Times like these give opportunity for the readjustment of emphasis of expenditure, the dropping of outlived organizations, "a clearing house." The business men of this generation are sometimes wiser than the children of light. The question may be asked as to whether money given for Missions is not sometimes used to support worthy but feeble clergymen in static parishes. There may be also discussions as to whether the Church, in order to spread the Gospel, has not spread out too thin; whether we are doing as effectively as we ought that we have set our hand to a generation ago; whether the small salaries of our missionaries do not hamper their usefulness and multiply cares. Shall a Diocese or Missionary District be given aid year after year which makes little effort to do its part for the general work of the Church? May this be not so much a sign of poverty as of inefficiency which suggests the waste in trying to aid?

After his resignation as Bishop of the Diocese of Massachusetts, while Bishop Lawrence by right retained his seat and vote in the House of Bishops, he took little part in the meetings of the House of Bishops. He attended only two special meetings, and for a few days only the General Convention in Atlantic City in 1934, and in Cincinnati in 1937. He did not go to the Convention in Denver in 1931, or in Kansas City in 1940. Once he had been considered somewhat of a stormy petrel in the House, pressing for such reforms as open sessions, and as late as 1923 his address "Fifty Years" created a considerable furore. To be sure, he had been elected Chairman of the House in 1904, and always was listened to with great attention and respect. As the years passed, he came to occupy seat No. 1 as the oldest Bishop in point of consecration. Debate came to mean less to him, and personal friendship more.

He had always recalled his own sense of shyness and loneliness when he had entered the House of Bishops in 1893. As a result, when he was at a General Convention, he always gave a dinner to the younger Bishops who had been consecrated within the previous three years, perhaps inviting two or three of the senior Bishops as speakers. These dinners were greatly enjoyed and brought him into personal touch with the younger men, who never forgot his friendly interest. At the Cincinnati Convention, he had the pleasure of presenting his son Appleton to the House of Bishops, and also he gave a brief address to the House of Clerical and Lay Delegates, as he happened to be visiting the Massachusetts delegation when a resolution praising the Church Pension Fund was adopted, and he was called upon to reply – a most unusual occurrence, for a Bishop rarely addresses a session of the other House.

He set his course of action in the House of Bishops by an address he was asked to give at the session in the Cathedral of St. John the Divine in 1927, when his resignation was accepted. It was an address moving in its simplicity, its directness, and its revelation of his character. He contrasted the personal religion of his later years with that of his earlier experience:

"What features stand out? The first is that of simplicity. As I get older, my faith becomes simpler: many elements of doctrine, ecclesiastical standards and practice which I once thought of essential importance have now fallen into the background; and I revert easily to childhood faith. Not that these other elements are not of importance, but with one's fuller experience and approach to the other life, the big essential simple truths are what I cling to and fall back upon.

"For instance, Trust in God as my Heavenly Father is the foundation of my faith. Trust as a child trusts. The clash of science and religion, the rough voices of ecclesiastical dispute are silent. God the Loving Father stands forth.

"My faith too has become more and more Christ-centered. I like to talk not first of Christianity but of Christ. Jesus, the humble, loving, strong Jesus catches my loyalty.

"And the Holy Spirit. He is not only a power or the

expression of a Power which fell upon the Apostles, but the Living Spirit of the Living God now, the Living Truth, invigorating and guiding the Church and the hearts of men: my heart and my life.

"Hence my personal religion is not that of the past, but of the present, real, practical, sustaining every day and every hour of the day.

"This leads to an increasing satisfaction in spiritual reality as expressed in spiritual character. My interest is less in the question as to where spiritual character comes from, or whether it is more or less exclusively in the Church and in Church people. Hence I find the fruits of the Spirit in men and women in every station of life, in every Church and in no church: in humility, purity, charity, truth, under an infinite variety of social groups, religious faiths, and racial skins. My attitude to those who neglect spiritual things is not, 'You are doing wrong,' but 'You are losing a fine chance.' "

The Bishop then touched upon his familiar subjects of the necessity of an avocation as one grows older, and of the significance of friendship.

He closed with a reference to St. John, and the power of love:

"The richest rewards of a long life are not found in wealth, fame, or even worthy admiration: they are found in the consciousness that one is loved, that he lives in the atmosphere of affection, and that all people of all sorts and conditions wish him well."

This thought was the substance of one of his last speeches in the House of Bishops. There was before the House a motion to take the right of a vote from retired Bishops.

Another distinguished elder Bishop defeated the measure by declaring that he came to vote and to assist by settling issues. Bishop Lawrence's statement was, "I have not voted since I retired, and I do not want a vote: those who are to execute the laws, the younger and active Bishops, should make the laws. As Bishops in this House, all are brothers on equal ground, but as lawmakers and executives we should have different responsibilities and powers: retired Bishops should not vote. Again this I count not a deprivation but a blessing. As a retired Bishop I want to be free from such, and able in old age to be a friend, pastor, and father-in-God to all sorts and conditions of people, and like the old Bishop at Ephesus to be able to say, 'Little children, love one another.' "

VII

The Last Year

THE span of Bishop Lawrence's life was indeed long. We gain some conception of its length when we realize that he was born a few weeks before the death of President Zachary Taylor and the accession of President Fillmore. As a boy he lived through the stirring days of the pre-war discussion of slavery and the preservation of the Union, in close touch with affairs through his father, who played an active part in the shaping of events. Then came the Civil War, and the days of so-called reconstruction, the growth and the development of the West, and the rise of the United States as a world power. A friend of Presidents Theodore Roosevelt and William H. Taft, he had intimate contact with our national life. Then came the first World War, the strange psychology of the post-war era — the period of false prosperity, and after it the depression. He watched and saw more clearly than most the threatening storm brewing in Europe, and he lived to within a month and a day of our entry into the second World War. No doubt every century will bring amazing changes, but it is doubtful if any one person will ever live to see more of the great transformations in the American way of life. What was true of the nation was equally true of the city of Boston, and of the Church. It is no wonder that Bishop Lawrence liked to recall the past. The wonder is that he consistently looked forward.

The Bishop's life was not merely long: it was remarkable in the realization of his hopes and dreams. We sometimes speak of a "well rounded" life. His was wonderfully so. He lived to see so many things "come to pass." Even if repetition is involved, it is worth mentioning some of these events.

The city of Lawrence, Kansas, had been named for the Bishop's father, because, to quote from a resolution of the Mayor and Commissioners of the city in 1929, it was Amos A. Lawrence's "great generosity and interest in the cause of freedom which was largely responsible for the successful founding of the city." The Bishop lived to see his father's role recognized in the seventy-fifth anniversary of the city, when the Bishop through his son Frederic presented a cup in memory of his father, and his father's portrait by Mrs. Peabody was hung in the hall of the University of Kansas, of which Amos A. Lawrence had been a benefactor.

He lived also to visit Lawrence College in Appleton, Wisconsin, another of his father's achievements, and to see the College give honorary degrees to his two sons. The same was true of the Seminary in Cambridge. He saw the little school in which his father had been interested develop into an important institution of theological learning, with generation after generation of future leaders of the Church passing through the portals of Lawrence Hall.

In his family, he had the joy of the arrival of children,

grandchildren, and great-grandchildren, and the satisfaction of witnessing their growth and development. He had the unusual privilege of consecrating his son Appleton as Bishop of a Diocese where he had once ministered as Bishop, which he had set apart, and for which he had raised the endowment. He lived to have a part in the great developments in his beloved University, to attend the Tercentenary, and to observe a new President in action. Before the end of his life, the Cathedral Church of St. Paul achieved his aim, and he was able to preach at the twenty-fifth anniversary of its founding. The Church Pension Fund had shown in twenty-four years its stability and its great service to the Church. Finally, in the month before his death, the cycle became complete when he instituted his son Frederic as Rector of St. Paul's Church, Brookline, the church he himself had attended as a little boy, and where he had sat on a stool drawing pictures while the Rector preached. In that institution, the home in Longwood became connected with the future ministry of his son. Few men are permitted so to see the accomplishment of their hopes.

The year 1941 opened with a premonition of serious illness, for he wrote on New Year's Day, "In house all day, as for several weeks I have had to be careful and go slow on account of slight heart warning." But he had always rallied before, and this time was no exception. He kept up with all his many contacts with family and friends, and engaged in a strenuous schedule for a man ninety years of age.

In the first months of the year, he offered prayer at the second inauguration of Governor Saltonstall; spoke for over two hours at a meeting of the Clericus Club, composed of Episcopal clergymen; was elected an honorary member of the Society of the Cincinnati and accepted with a speech; addressed a meeting of the Church Home Society; gave an address over the radio entitled "Defense of America"; made the prayer at the one hundred and fiftieth anniversary of the Massachusetts Historical Society; and spoke to a gathering of Red Cross workers. Certainly this does not give any indication of "slowing up."

For his ninety-first birthday, there was a happy company of family and friends at Mrs. Reed's, including Mrs. Theodore Roosevelt, Senior. "I had not seen her since her years in the White House and Theodore. We had a good talk on old times. As she left, she said, 'I have had such a good time.'" On this trip, he baptized two great-grandchildren.

Returning to Boston, he addressed the graduating class at the Episcopal Theological School Commencement and attended a reception to the Crown Princess Juliana of Holland in the School Library. The next day he had the great joy of taking part in the Service of Ordination to the Diaconate of his grandson, Charles Kane Cobb Lawrence, at St. Peter's Church in Cambridge.

Shortly there followed the Harvard Commencement, at which he received the Harvard Alumni Award. On that occasion he stood straight as an arrow, and with clear, strong voice expressed his appreciation, humorously corrected Governor Saltonstall upon the number of Commencements he had attended, and told of the Commencement of 1862. The *Harvard Alumni Bulletin* described the scene, "Touched to the heart, and touching the hearts of all, he stood at ninety-one before the throng in the friendly simplicity with which he would have met any single member of it."

The summer was spent as usual at Bar Harbor, with happy gatherings of the family and of friends. In July, the new Bishop of Maine, the Rt. Rev. Oliver Loring, came to visit the Church of Our Saviour. Bishop Loring's father had for many years until his death been Rector of St. John's Church, Newtonville, so Bishop Lawrence had watched Oliver Loring grow up, and was delighted to be able to welcome him in a short address. Later they were photographed together in their robes – the oldest and the youngest Bishops of the Church.

Bishop Lawrence returned to Readville early in September. In that month he baptized another great-grandchild, and on September 28 instituted Fred as Rector of St. Paul's Church, Brookline, in his address recalling the days of his childhood, and then stressing the opportunity before the Church today, particularly in regard to enlisting the interest of young people.

October fifth marked the forty-eighth anniversary of his consecration as Bishop. He attended service at Fred's church, and for the last time of many entered in his diary the number of his descendants.

> Forty-eighth anniversary of my consecration. Very happy year: death of Julia my one great loss. More blessings than anyone ever had. Have now seven living children, twenty-seven grandchildren, and eight great-grandchildren.

In October, he spoke at the matriculation dinner of the School in Cambridge, and made a brief address at the one hundredth anniversary of St. John's Church, Jamaica Plain. In that month's *Church Militant* he had an article called

"Are We Alert?" Already he saw that the war was at hand.

"The fact stands before us that our Nation is in danger, in real danger of losing the very principles that made her what she is – in danger of her very life. Though many are still questioning, others doubting and postponing, the great body of the people have been convinced that we as a Nation must put up a defense which will meet and overcome any attack. Hence the call to action – to action based on conviction that if liberties and spiritual riches are to be held secure, every citizen must place his comfort, his wealth and his life at its service."

Bishop Lawrence must have been feeling well, for on October 29 he introduced the Rt. Rev. Ronald Hall, Bishop of Hong Kong, to a luncheon meeting at the City Club in aid of United China Relief; and the next afternoon saw with Miss Cunningham the current play, "Arsenic and Old Lace." On Sunday, November 2, he instituted the Rev. David Hunter as Rector of the Church of the Holy Spirit, Mattapan. On Tuesday, November 4, he recorded, "To Boston to vote for Mayor."

The last entry in his diary was on November 5, and reads, "Tobin re-elected Mayor by 9,000 majority." That night he was taken ill with a heart attack, and the end came the following day. It was as he would have wished, in the midst of a keen interest in life, with no weakening of faculties, and a short illness. We are reminded of his words, true to the end: "In perfect faith one may live on toward the setting of the sun, tranquil and in perfect serenity."

At once there were countless expressions of sorrow, and of the respect and affection in which he was held by a great multitude. The flags of the City and State were at half-mast. The newspapers printed columns of description of his long and useful life, and messages of sympathy to the family poured in from all over the country. Later on, the Church press and the *Harvard Alumni Bulletin* paid tribute to the Bishop, as did the many groups with which he had been associated. President Lowell wrote, "Only genius has the scope to write an epitaph for such a man."

As he had requested, the funeral service was held at the Cathedral Church of St. Paul, which was so crowded that the throng reached out onto the Common across Tremont Street. Present were Bishops and clergy, representatives of the State and of the City, of Harvard University, of the Church Pension Fund, and a great company of friends and associates of the years. The service was conducted by the Bishop of the Diocese, the Dean of the Cathedral, Dr. Endicott Peabody, and the Presiding Bishop, the Rt. Rev. Henry St. George Tucker, who pronounced the Benediction. The entire service spoke not of death but of life. The great congregation joined in the General Thanksgiving, and in the singing of the triumphant hymns, "There's a wideness in God's mercy," "The strife is o'er," and especially Julia Ward Howe's, "Mine eyes have seen the glory of the coming of the Lord," reminiscent of the events of his boyhood and of the family gatherings on Sunday evenings at Bar Harbor. "Peace, perfect peace" was a reminder of the Bishop's own serene faith. It is certain that if he could have made another entry that evening in his diary, it would have read, "Very beautiful."

The funeral procession went by the University he had served so long, and stopped at the School for a brief service of prayer, conducted by Dean Dun in St. John's Chapel, and then continued on to Mount Auburn, where Appleton and Fred conducted the Service of Committal. The Bishop's body was laid beside that of his beloved Julia.

Today a simple stone monument stands there, with the inscription,

William Lawrence
Seventh Bishop of Massachusetts
Born May 30, 1850
Died November 6, 1941

and then the words in which a great company join as they thank God for his life, and which were so often on his own lips:

Bless the Lord, O my Soul.

INDEX

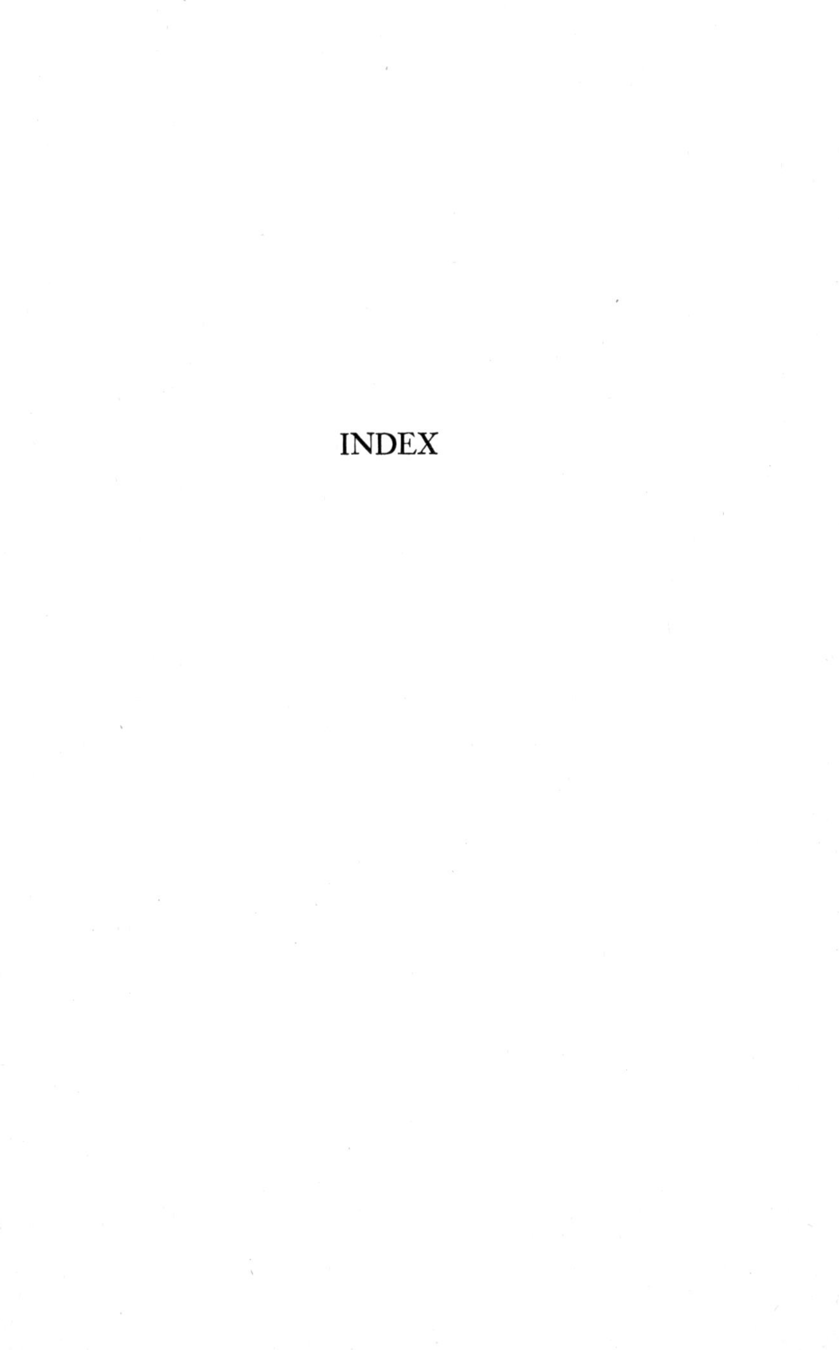

INDEX